CORE English 小学 3 年　この本の使い方

この本は，３年生でみにつけておきたい英語の語句や表現に慣れ親しみ，使えるようになるためのテキストです。たくさんの音声を聞きながら，本誌とワークブックに取り組むことで，将来につながる確かな英語力がみにつきます。
音声は繰り返し何度も聞いて，マネをして言ってみましょう。

この本の構成

Unit

英語の基本的な語彙と表現を学びます。1Unit は6ページ構成となっています。別冊のワークブックも同じく6ページ構成で見開き対応しています。テキストと一緒に使いましょう。
Key Words では，おぼえておきたい語彙をイラストとともに提示しています。
Listen and Talk で，それらの語彙を使った会話を聞きます。場面をしめしたイラストを見ながら聞くことで，どんな内容なのか理解することができます。十分に聞いたら Role-play をしてみましょう。
More Words で，別のカテゴリーの語彙にも親しみます。
Listening Activity では，More Words の語彙を扱った音声を聞いて，内容をとらえる練習ができます。
Song には，それぞれの Unit で学んだ表現を取り入れた英語の歌を収録しています。歌詞を見ながら聞いて練習し，歌ってみましょう。
Learn Some More は，反対の意味を表す言葉を学びます。
Listen to Your Teacher は教室でよく使われる表現を取り上げています。先生の英語の指示にあわせて動けるように練習しましょう。
Alphabet Activity では，９Unit を通じてアルファベットの大文字を書く力を養います。

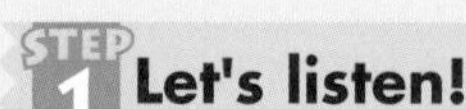
STEP 1
Let's listen!

CD1
1
自然な速さで読まれた英語を聞いてみましょう。
文字を見ながら聞きましょう。

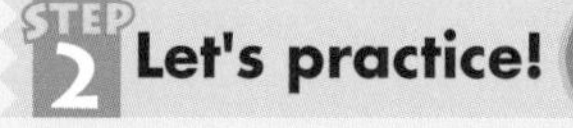
STEP 2
Let's practice!

CD1
2
お手本に続いてリピート発声しながら発話練習をします。

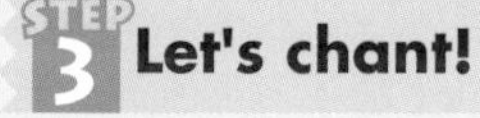
STEP 3
Let's chant!

CD1
3
チャンツで発話練習をします。
何度も聞いて，マネをして言ってみましょう。

Review

3Unit ごとに入る，まとめのページです。
前に学習したことをおぼえているか，確認してみましょう。

操作が簡単なデジタルブックで英語の音声を繰り返し聞こう！

①右下にある QR コードでデジタルブックにアクセス。
②もくじから見たい Unit をタップ。
③ページ移動は，両端の黒いところをタップ。音声を聞くには，CD のアイコンをタップ。

Unit 2
How are you?
Key Words
fine
good
great
hungry
thirsty
sleepy
tired
happy
Listen and Talk
Good morning. How are you?
I'm fine.
I'm sleepy.
I'm good.
How are you? Are you tired?
I'm great.
I'm tired.
I'm thirsty.

<動作環境> Google Chrome / Safari(Mac)
インターネットに接続できる環境が必要です。
Wi-Fi での使用をオススメします。

JN125240

CORE English 小学 3 年 もくじ

このテキストに出てくるキャラクター

日本の小学校で学ぶ
Mayu, Shohei,
Anna, Hasan
Anna はロシア出身の女の子
Hasan はトルコ出身の男の子

写真提供：PIXTA（ピクスタ）

アメリカのボストンに住むLisa と Ken の家族
日本に住むおじいちゃんおばあちゃんや友だちとビデオチャットを楽しんでいる。

Unit 1

■いろいろな言語のあいさつと，名前や住んでいる国の紹介のしかたに慣れ親しむ
■スポーツの言い方と，好きなスポーツを伝える表現に慣れ親しむ

Hello!

Listen and Talk　いろいろな国のあいさつを聞いてみよう！

STEP 1 Let's listen! 

STEP 2 Let's practice! 

Hello, I'm Lisa.
Hi, I'm Ken.
We live in America.
Nice to meet you.

音声を聞いて練習した回数にあわせて，花びらを１枚ずつぬりましょう。

STEP 1 Let's listen!

CD1 3
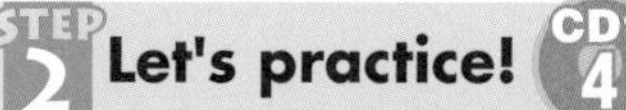
STEP 2 Let's practice!
CD1 4
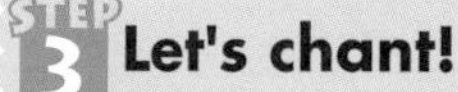
STEP 3 Let's chant!

CD1 5

International Day

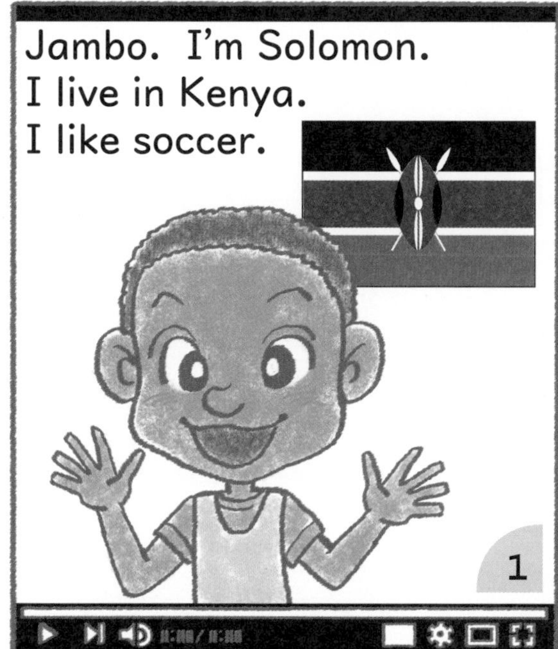
Jambo. I'm Solomon.
I live in Kenya.
I like soccer.
1

你好。My name is Linly.
I live in China.
I like table tennis.
2

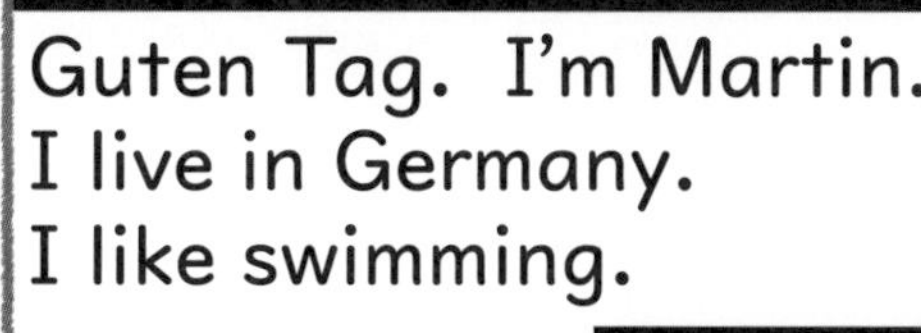
Guten Tag. I'm Martin.
I live in Germany.
I like swimming.

3

Bonjour. I'm Emma.
I live in France.
I like tennis.
4

More Words

スポーツの言い方をおぼえよう！

STEP 1 Let's listen! CD1 6　STEP 2 Let's practice! CD1 7　STEP 3 Let's chant! CD1 8

① 

soccer

② 

tennis

③ 

swimming

④ 

baseball

⑤ 

dodgeball

⑥ 

volleyball

⑦ 

basketball

⑧ 

table tennis

⑨ 

badminton

Listening Activity

英語(えいご)を聞いて，それぞれがどのスポーツを好(す)きか，上のイラストの番号(ばんごう)を書こう。

① 

② 

③ 

④ 

Song 英語の歌を聞いて，歌ってみよう！

STEP 1 Let's listen! CD1 10　STEP 2 Let's practice!  STEP 3 Let's sing! 

What Sport Do You Like?

Soccer, swimming, table tennis,
badminton, and tennis.
What sport do you like?
I like soccer.
I like swimming.
I like table tennis.
How about you?

Dodgeball, baseball,
basketball, and volleyball.
What sport do you like?
I like dodgeball.
I like baseball.
I like basketball.
How about you?

対になる言葉を聞いてみよう！

STEP 1 Let's listen! 

STEP 2 Let's practice! 

① 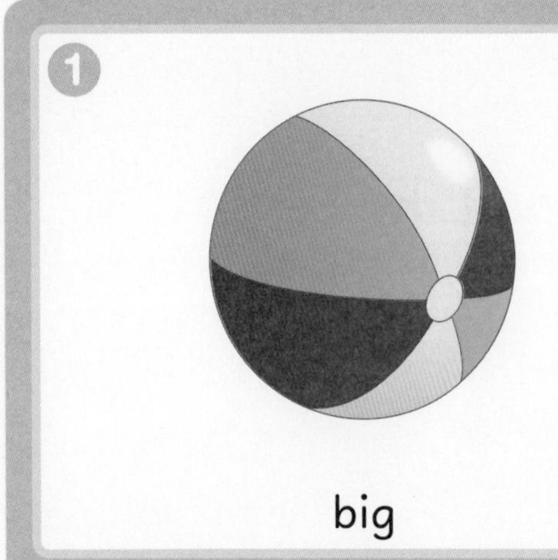

big

② 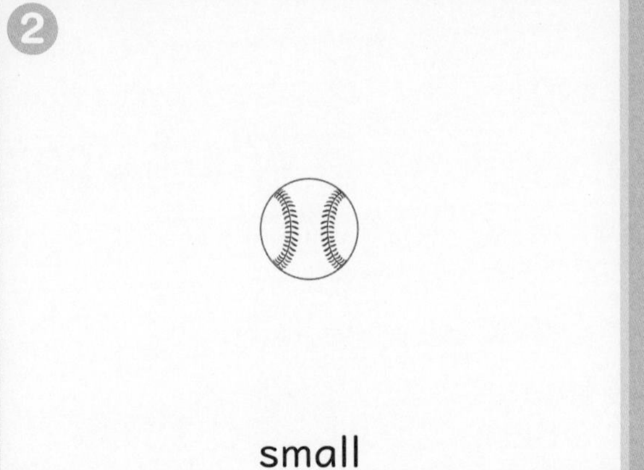

small

Listen to Your Teacher

英語を聞いて，言われた動作をしてみよう！

STEP 1 Let's listen! 

STEP 2 Let's practice! 

① 

Stand up, please.

② 

Sit down, please.

③ 

Raise your hand.

④ 

Put your hand down.

Alphabet Activity

アルファベットソングを歌おう。

STEP 1 Let's sing! 

 Let's practice! 

A alligator

B balloon

C cake

D donut

E eggplant

F frog

G goat

H helicopter

I igloo

J jet

K key

L ladybug

M monkey

N net

O otter

P pizza

Q quiz

R robot

S seven

T ten

U undershirt

V van

W watch

X six

Y yarn

Z zero

アルファベットソングの楽譜は p.70〜72にあります。見ながら歌ってみましょう。

Unit 2

□感情や状態を表す言い方に慣れ親しみ，相手の様子をたずねたり答えたりする
□食べ物の言い方と，好きな食べ物を伝える表現に慣れ親しむ

How are you?

Key Words

気持(きも)ちや状態(じょうたい)を表(あらわ)す言い方をおぼえよう！

STEP 1 Let's listen! 

STEP 2 Let's practice! 

STEP 3 Let's chant! 

① 
fine

② 
good

③ 
great

④ 
hungry

⑤ 
thirsty

⑥ 
sleepy

⑦ 
tired

⑧ 
happy

⑨ 
sad

Listen and Talk 気持ちや状態についての会話を聞いてみよう！

STEP 1 Let's listen! CD1 22　STEP 2 Let's practice! CD1 23　STEP 3 Let's chant! CD1 24

1

Good morning. How are you?
I'm fine.
I'm sleepy.
I'm good.

2

How are you? Are you tired?
I'm great.
I'm tired.
I'm thirsty.

Role-play 10ページのイラストを見ながら単語(たんご)を入れ替(か)えて，気持ちや状態について会話してみよう。

 How are you?

 I'm [fine].

More Words

食べ物や飲み物の言い方をおぼえよう！

STEP 1 Let's listen! 
STEP 2 Let's practice! 
STEP 3 Let's chant! 

① 
toast

② 

cereal

③ 
salad

④ 

jam

⑤ 
cheese

⑥ 

milk

⑦ 
orange juice

⑧ 
cake

⑨ 
pudding

Listening Activity

英語を聞いて，それぞれがどの食べ物を好きか，上のイラストの番号を書こう。

CD1 28

① 

② 

③ 

④ 

Song 英語の歌を聞いて，歌ってみよう！

STEP 1 Let's listen! CD1 29　STEP 2 Let's practice! CD1 30　STEP 3 Let's sing! CD1 31

Hello! How Are You?

Hello! Hello! Hello! How are you?
I'm good. I'm great. I'm happy.
Hello! Hello! Hello! How are you?
I'm fine, thank you. And you?

Hello! Hello! Hello! How are you?
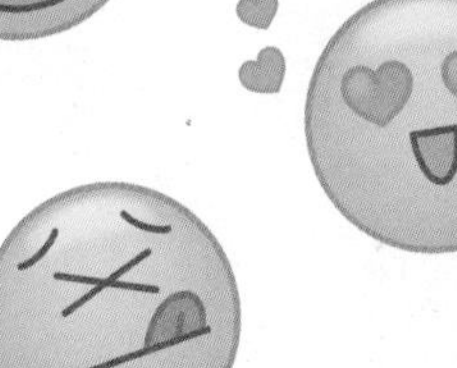
I'm hungry. I'm thirsty.
Hello! Hello! Hello! How are you?

I'm very sad today.

Hello! Hello! Hello! How are you?

I'm sleepy. I'm tired.
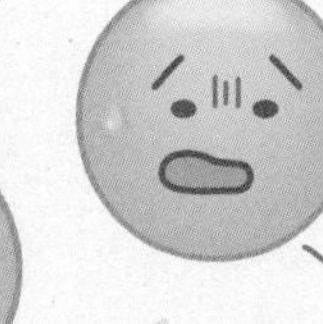
Hello! Hello! Hello! How are you?
I'm not so good today.

Learn Some More

対になる言葉を聞いてみよう！

STEP 1 Let's listen! CD1 32

STEP 2 Let's practice! CD1 33

①

yummy

②

yucky

Listen to Your Teacher

英語を聞いて，言われた動作をしてみよう！

STEP 1 Let's listen! CD1 34

STEP 2 Let's practice! CD1 35

①

Take out your textbook.

②

Put your textbook away.

③

Pick up your pencil.

④

Put your pencil down.

Alphabet Activity

アルファベットソングを歌おう。
英語を聞いて，かくれている大文字に○をつけよう。

STEP 1 Let's sing! CD1 36

STEP 2 Let's practice! CD1 37

Unit 3

□ 1から20までの数に慣れ親しみ，足し算・引き算の問題を出したり答えたりする
□ 文房具の言い方と，文房具がいくつあるかたずねたり答えたりする表現に慣れ親しむ

How many?

Key Words

1から20までの数の言い方をおぼえよう！

STEP 1 Let's listen!  STEP 2 Let's practice!  STEP 3 Let's chant! 

one

two

three

four

five

six

seven

eight

nine

ten

eleven

twelve

thirteen

fourteen

fifteen

sixteen

seventeen

eighteen

nineteen

twenty

 Listen and Talk

足し算・引き算についての会話を聞いてみよう！

STEP 1 Let's listen! CD2 4　　STEP 2 Let's practice! CD2 5　　STEP 3 Let's chant! CD2 6

1

2

Role-play 英語で足し算・引き算の問題を出しあって，会話してみよう。

 What is [8] plus [9]?

 [8] plus [9] is [17].

 What is [20] minus [3]?

 [20] minus [3] is [17].

More Words

文房具(ぶんぼうぐ)がいくつあるか，数えて言ってみよう！

STEP 1 Let's listen! 
STEP 2 Let's practice! 
STEP 3 Let's chant! 

①  
rulers

② 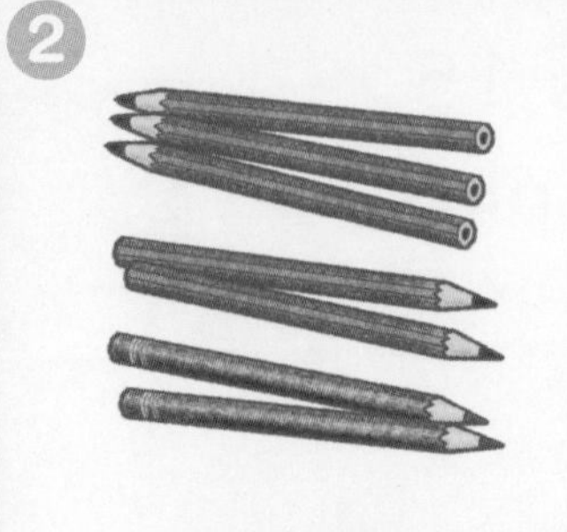
pencils

③ 
crayons

④ 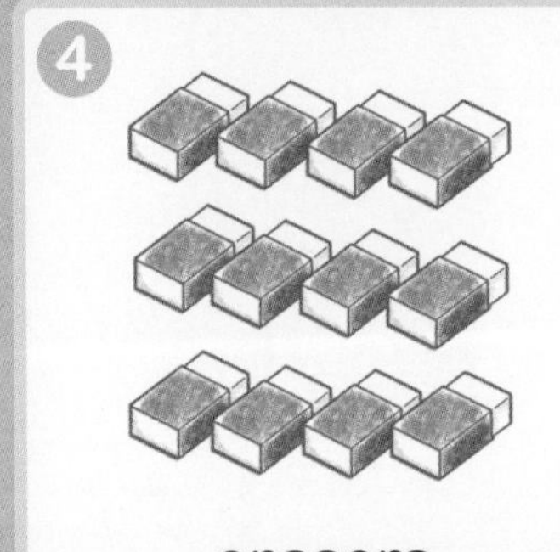
erasers

⑤ 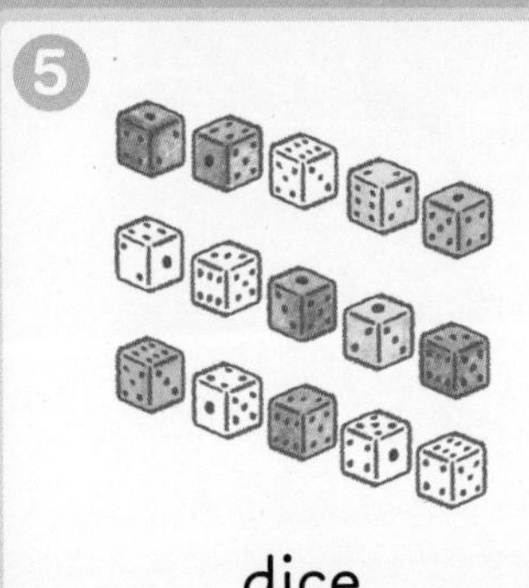
dice

⑥ 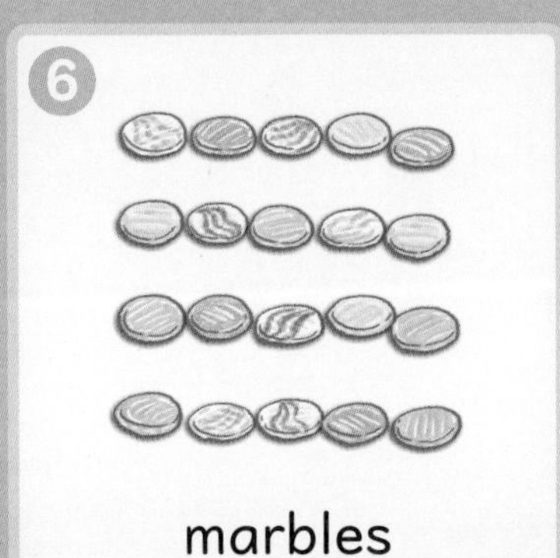
marbles

Listening Activity

上のイラストを見ながら文房具の数をたずねる会話を聞いて，答えを数字で書こう。

CD2 10

How many ＿＿＿＿?

① 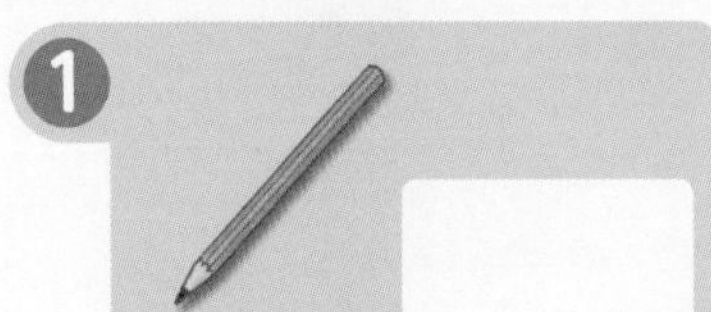

② 

③ 

④ 

⑤ 

⑥ 

Song

英語の歌を聞いて，歌ってみよう！

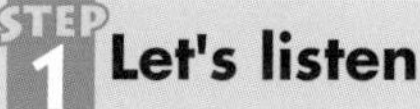

STEP 1 Let's listen! CD2 11

STEP 2 Let's practice! CD2 12

STEP 3 Let's sing! CD2 13

1 2 3 4 5 Once I Caught a Fish Alive

One Two Three Four Five

Once I caught a fish alive.

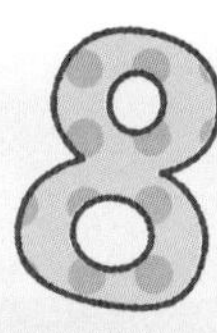

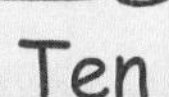

Six Seven Eight Nine Ten

Then I let it go again.

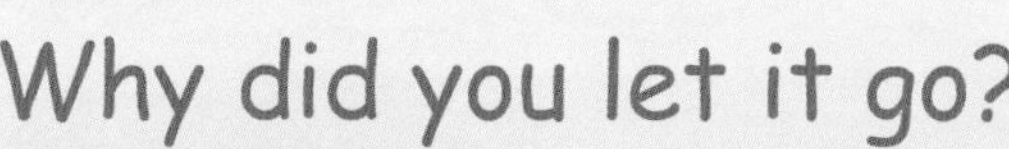

Why did you let it go?

Because it bit my finger so.

Which finger did it bite?

This little finger on the right.

Learn Some More 対になる言葉を聞いてみよう！

STEP 1 Let's listen!  STEP 2 Let's practice! 

① 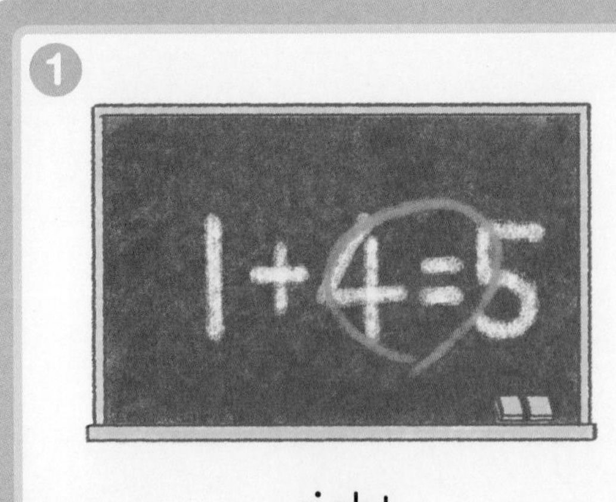

right

② 

wrong

Listen to Your Teacher 英語を聞いて，言われた動作をしてみよう！

STEP 1 Let's listen!  STEP 2 Let's practice! 

① 
Open your textbook.

② 
Close your textbook.

③ 
Give me five!

④ 
Give me ten!

Alphabet Activity

アルファベットソングを歌おう。
英語を聞いて，A から Z まで線でむすぼう。

STEP 1 Let's sing! CD2 18

STEP 2 Let's practice! CD2 19

Review 1 Unit 1-3

1 (1)と(2)の自己紹介を聞いて，内容にあうイラストに○をつけましょう。

(1)

I like ______ ______.

I like ______ ______.

(2)

I like ______ ______.

I like ______ ______.

2 (1)と(2)の対話を聞いて，内容にあうイラストに○をつけましょう。

(1)  How many erasers, Shohei?

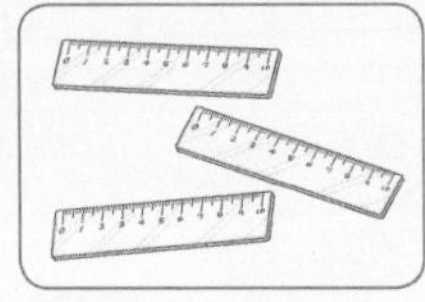

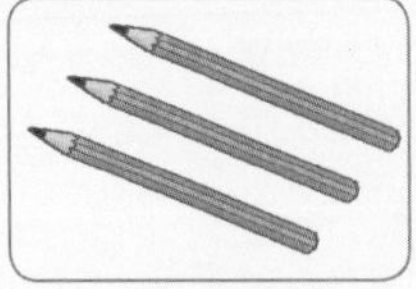

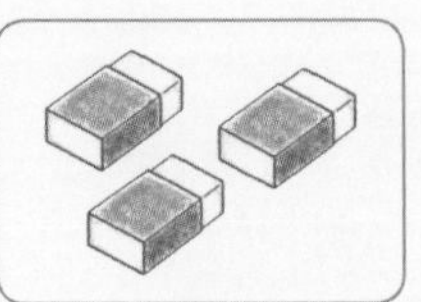

---

(2) What is thirteen plus eleven?

14	24	4

3 (1)～(4)の会話を聞いて，内容にあうイラストを下からえらんで，A から D の記号を□に書きましょう。 CD2 22

(1) □ (2) □ (3) □ (4) □

4 英語を聞いて，内容にあうイラストの□に✓をつけましょう。 CD2 23

(1)

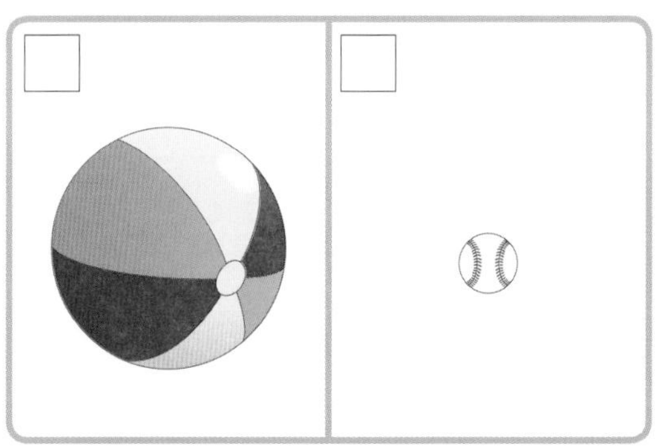

(2)

(3)

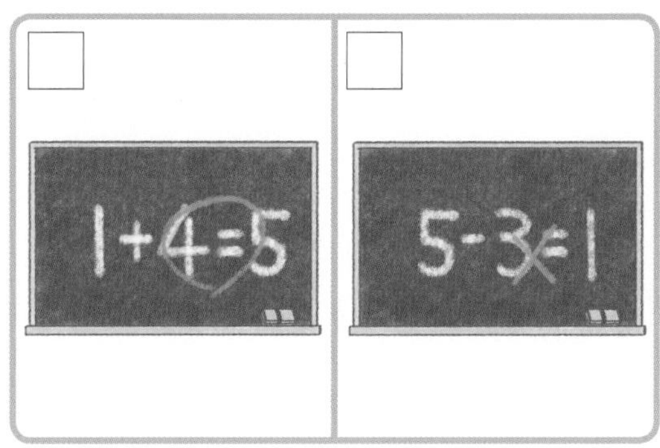

(4)

Unit 4

□色の言い方に慣れ親しみ，好みの色をたずねたり，Yes/No で答えたりする
□野菜の言い方と，野菜の好みをたずねたり答えたりする表現に慣れ親しむ

I like blue.

Key Words 色の言い方をおぼえよう！

STEP 1 Let's listen! CD2 24　STEP 2 Let's practice! CD2 25　STEP 3 Let's chant! CD2 26

① 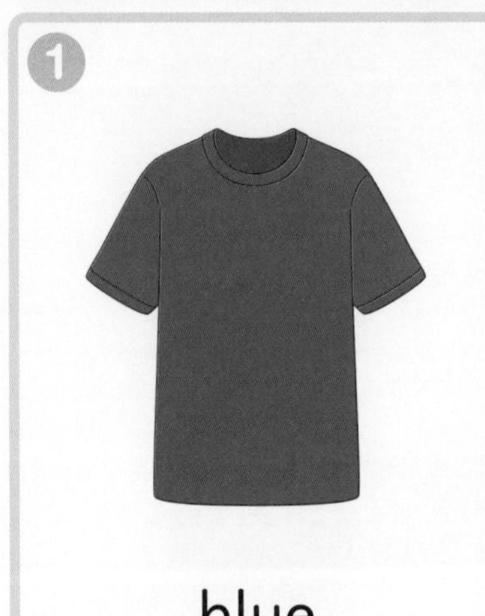
blue

② 
black

③ 
yellow

④ 
pink

⑤ 
white

⑥ 
purple

⑦ 
red

⑧ 
brown

⑨ 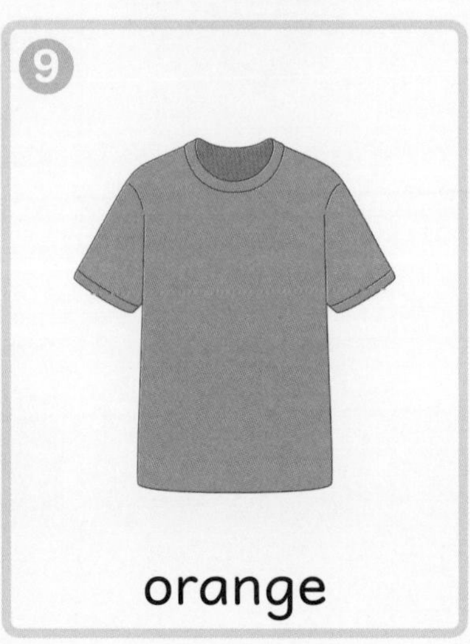
orange

Listen and Talk

好きな色についての会話を聞いてみよう！

STEP 1 Let's listen! CD2 27　STEP 2 Let's practice! CD2 28　STEP 3 Let's chant! CD2 29

1

Look! Pretty colors!
Do you like purple?
Yes, I do.
How about you?
I like orange.

2

Wow, lots of colors!
Do you like red?
No, I don't.
I don't like red. I like blue.

Role-play 24ページのイラストを見ながら単語を入れ替えて，好きな色について会話してみよう。

Do you like [blue]?

Yes, I do.

No, I don't. I don't like [blue].
I like [red].

More Words

野菜の言い方をおぼえよう！

STEP 1 Let's listen! CD2 30　　STEP 2 Let's practice! CD2 31　　STEP 3 Let's chant! CD2 32

1
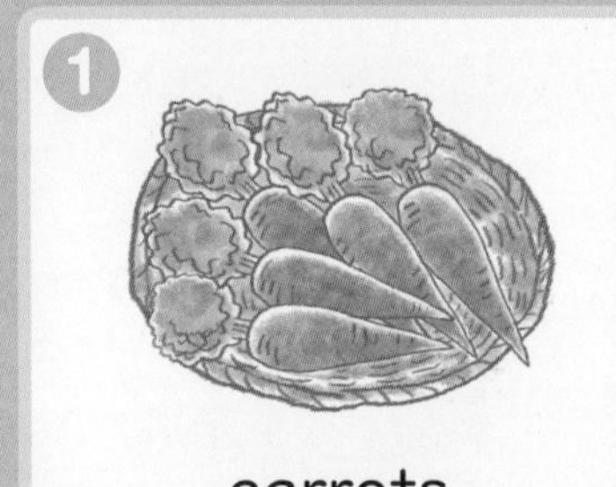
carrots

2

eggplants

3

onions

4

pumpkins

5
mushrooms

6

cucumbers

7

green peppers

8
tomatoes

9

sweet potatoes

Listening Activity

会話を聞いて，それぞれがどの野菜を好きか，
上のイラストの番号を書こう。

1

2

3

4

Song 英語の歌を聞いて，歌ってみよう！

STEP 1 Let's listen! CD2 34　STEP 2 Let's practice! CD2 35　STEP 3 Let's sing! CD2 36

I Like the Blue Shirt

Do you like the blue shirt?
Yes, I do.
I like the red shirt, too.
Do you like the brown shirt?
No, I don't.
I don't like the brown shirt.

Do you like the blue jeans?
Yes, I do.
I like the black jeans, too.
Do you like the yellow pants?
No, I don't.
I don't like the yellow pants.

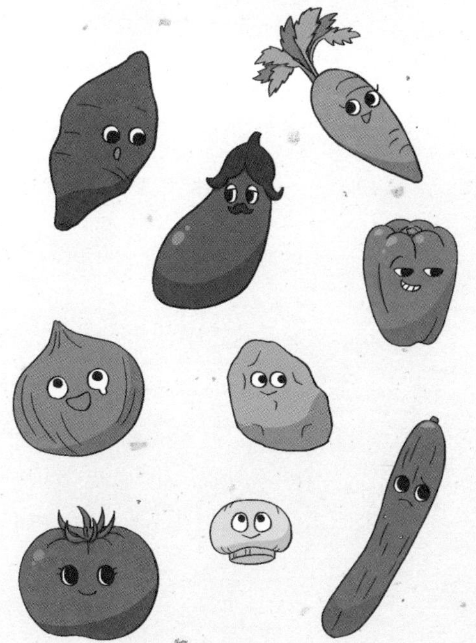

Do you like sweet potatoes?
Yes, I do.
I like eggplants, too.
Do you like green peppers?
No, I don't.
I don't like green peppers.

Do you like onions?
Yes, I do.
I like mushrooms, too.
Do you like cucumbers?
No, I don't.
I don't like cucumbers.

Learn Some More 対になる言葉を聞いてみよう！

STEP 1 Let's listen! CD2 37　STEP 2 Let's practice! CD2 38

1

old

2

new

Listen to Your Teacher 英語を聞いて，言われた動作をしてみよう！

STEP 1 Let's listen! CD2 39　STEP 2 Let's practice! 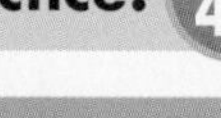

1

Draw a picture.

2

Color the picture.

3

Trace the letters.

4

Write the letters.

Alphabet Activity

アルファベットソングを歌おう。
英語を聞いて，A から Z まで順にたどってゴールしよう。

STEP 1 Let's sing! CD2 41　STEP 2 Let's practice! CD2 42

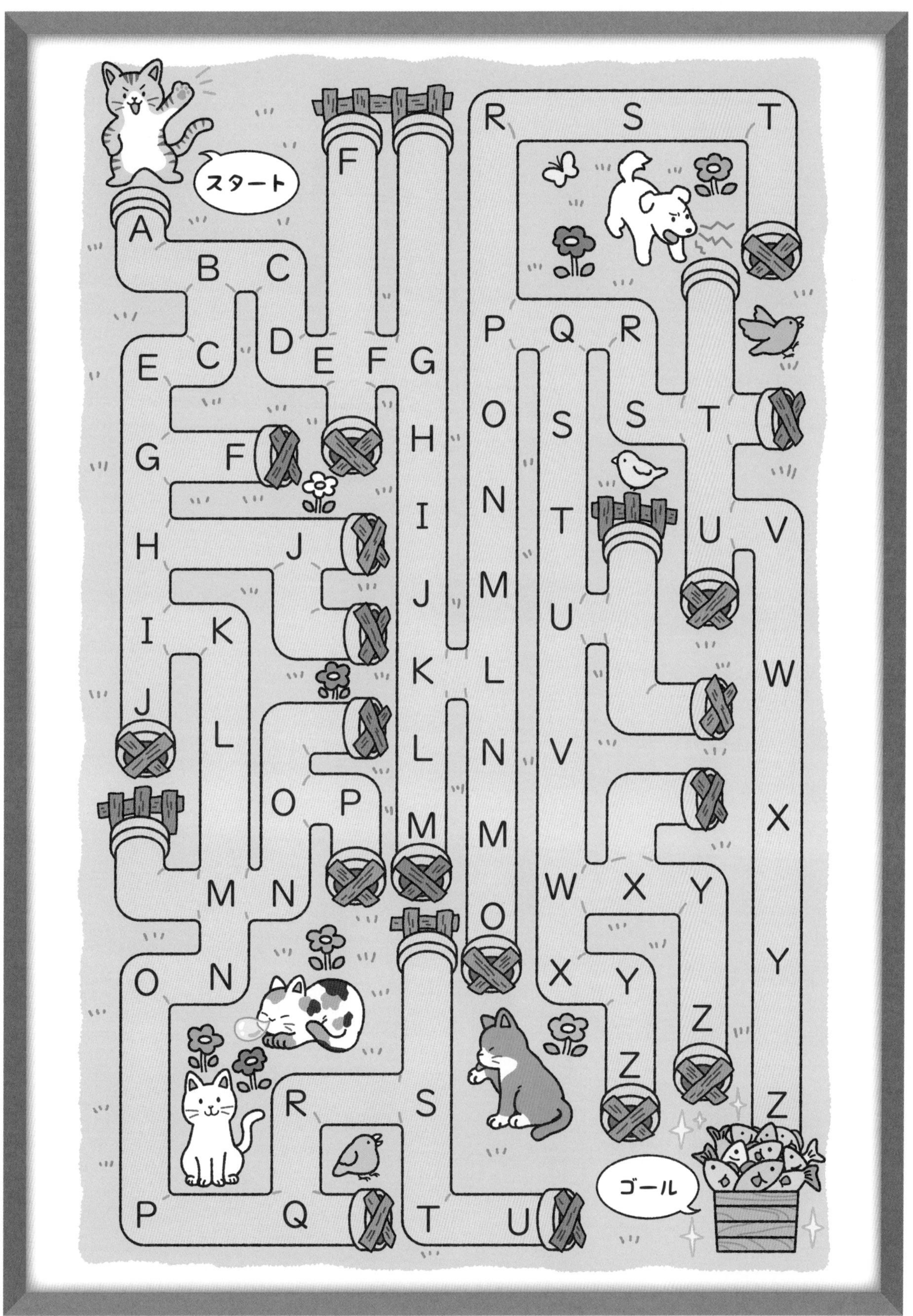

Unit 5 ■食べ物の言い方に慣れ親しみ，どの食べ物が好きかたずねたり答えたりする
■果物の言い方と，どの果物が好きかたずねたり答えたりする表現に慣れ親しむ

What food do you like?

Key Words 食べ物の言い方をおぼえよう！

STEP 1 Let's listen! CD3 1 

STEP 2 Let's practice! CD3 2 

STEP 3 Let's chant! CD3 3 

① 
chocolate

② 
pudding

③ 
ice cream

④ 
rice

⑤ 
bread

⑥ 
pizza

⑦ 
cheese

⑧ 
spaghetti

⑨ 
fried chicken

⑩ 
noodles

⑪ 
hamburgers

⑫ 
sandwiches

Listen and Talk 好きな食べ物についての会話を聞いてみよう！

STEP 1 Let's listen!  CD3 4　STEP 2 Let's practice! CD3 5　STEP 3 Let's chant!  CD3 6

1

2

Role-play 30ページのイラストを見ながら単語を入れ替えて，好きな食べ物について会話してみよう。

 What food do you like?

 I like [pizza]. How about you?

 I like [noodles].

More Words

果物(くだもの)の言い方をおぼえよう！

STEP 1 Let's listen! CD3 7 
STEP 2 Let's practice! CD3 8 
STEP 3 Let's chant! CD3 9 

① 
apples

② 
bananas

③ 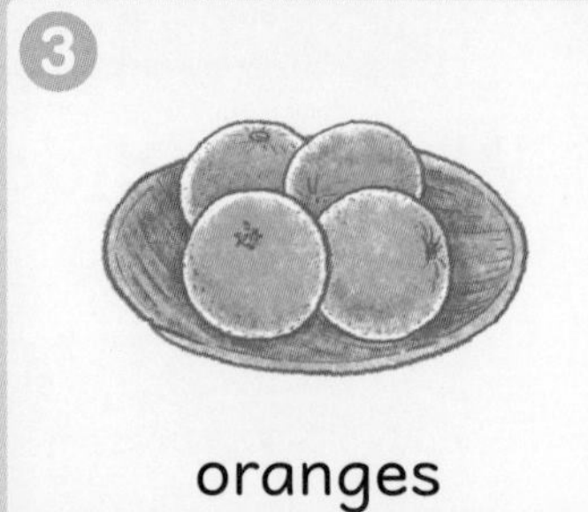
oranges

④ 
persimmons

⑤ 
pears

⑥ 
cherries

⑦ 
strawberries

⑧ 
peaches

⑨ 
grapes

Listening Activity

英語を聞いて，それぞれがどの果物を好きか，
上のイラストの番号を書こう。

CD3 10 

① 

② 

③ 

④ 

Song 英語の歌を聞いて，歌ってみよう！

STEP 1 Let's listen!  CD3 11　STEP 2 Let's practice! CD3 12　STEP 3 Let's sing! CD3 13

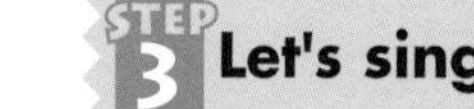

What Do You Like?

Fried chicken, hamburgers, spaghetti, and pizza.
What do you like?
What do you like?
I like fried chicken.
I like spaghetti.
How about you?
How about you?

Ice cream, pudding, chocolate, and cheese.
What do you like?
What do you like?
I like ice cream.
I like chocolate.
How about you?
How about you?

Strawberries, persimmons, pears, and peaches.
What do you like?
What do you like?
I like persimmons.
I like peaches.
How about you?
How about you?

Learn Some More 対になる言葉を聞いてみよう！

STEP 1 Let's listen!  STEP 2 Let's practice! CD3 15

①

fast

②

slow

Listen to Your Teacher 英語を聞いて，言われた動作をしてみよう！

STEP 1 Let's listen!  STEP 2 Let's practice! 

①

Look at the picture.

②
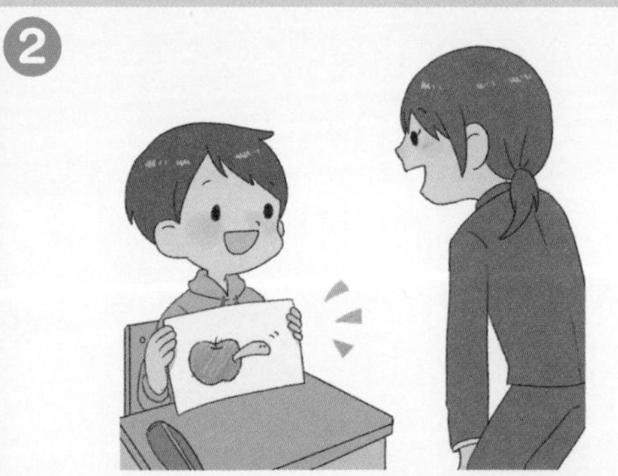
Show me your picture.

③

Point to the letter A.

④

Touch the letter A.

Alphabet Activity

アルファベットソングを歌おう。
英語を聞いて，大文字を完成(かんせい)させよう。

1 英語を聞きながら，反対側(はんたいがわ)をかがみのように書いて大文字を完成させましょう。

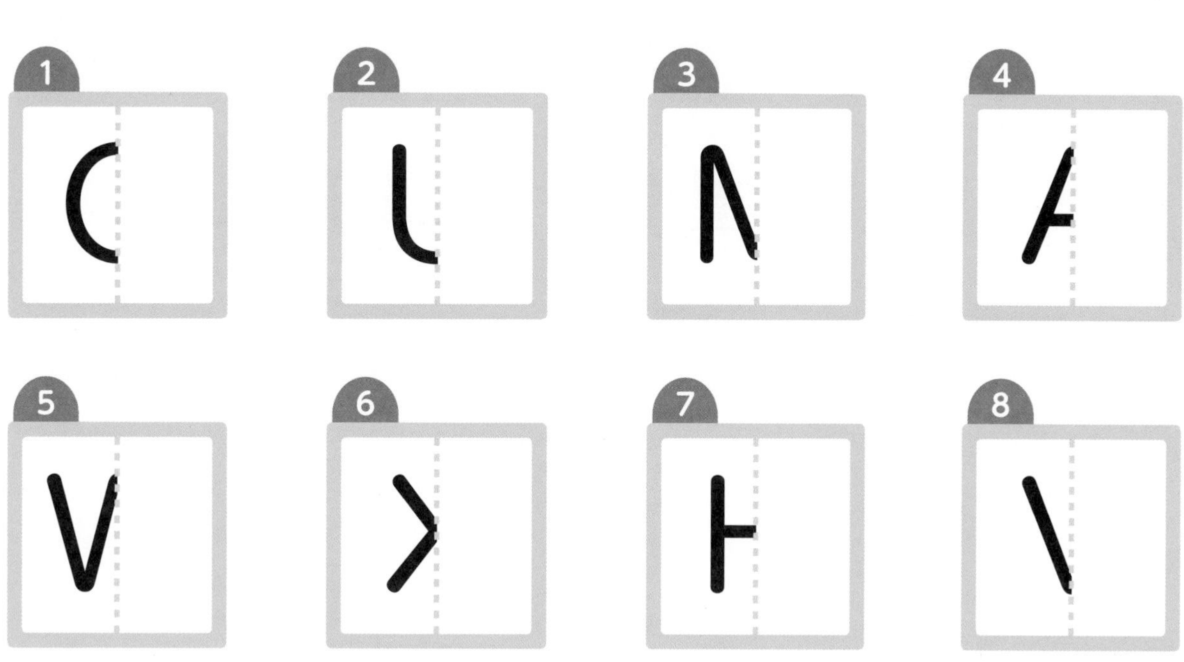

2 英語を聞きながら，欠(か)けているところを足して大文字を完成させましょう。

STEP 2 Let's practice! CD3 20

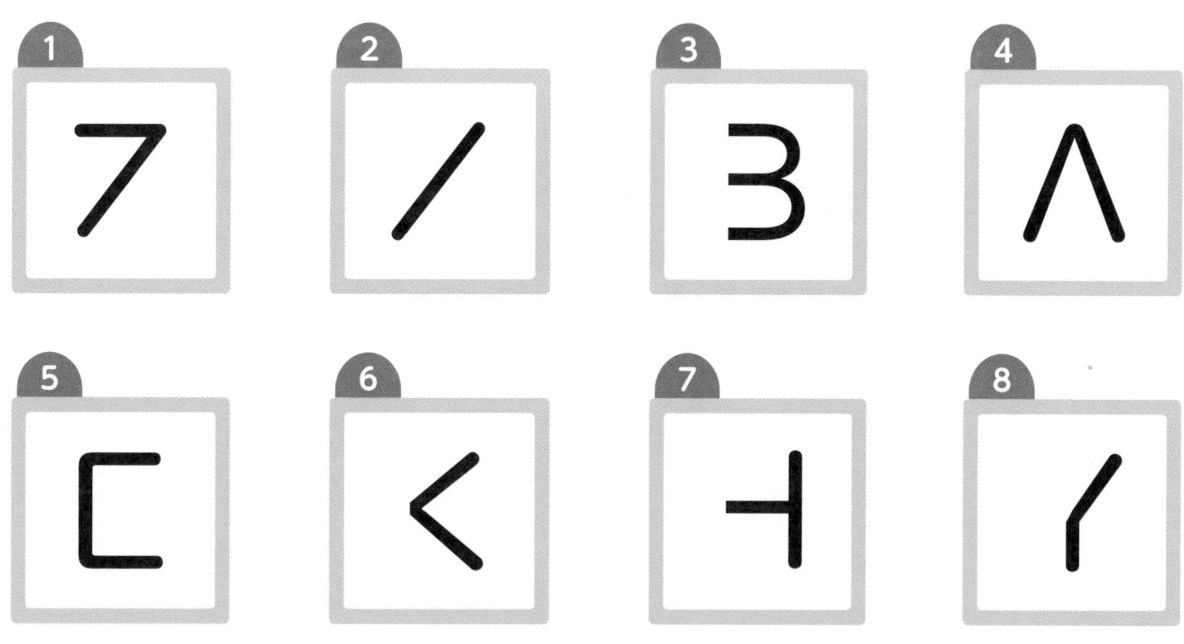

■アルファベットの大文字で書かれた数の文字数を答えたり，大文字を読んだりする
■時刻をたずねたり答えたりする表現に慣れ親しむ

Numbers and the Alphabet

Key Words

数字を表すアルファベットの大文字を読んでみよう！

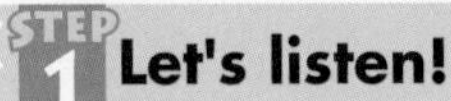

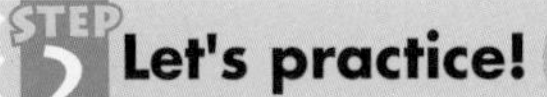

STEP 3 Let's chant!

Number Chart

Listen and Talk

数字とアルファベットの大文字についての会話を聞いてみよう！

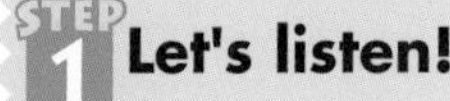
STEP 1 Let's listen!

CD3 24

STEP 2 Let's practice! CD3 25

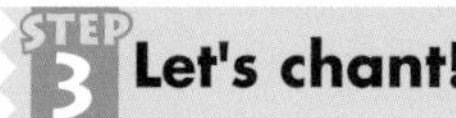
STEP 3 Let's chant!

CD3 26

1

Look at No.1 on the Number Chart.
How many letters of the alphabet can you see?
Number Chart
1 ONE
2 TWO
3 THREE
4 FOUR
5 FIVE
6 SIX
7 SEVEN
8 EIGHT
9 NINE
3 letters.
That's right!

2

Role-play 36ページのイラストを見て，数字とアルファベットの大文字について会話してみよう。

Look at No. 2.
How many letters of the alphabet can you see?

3 letters.

Can you name the letters?

T, W, O.

More Words

時刻の言い方をおぼえよう！

STEP 1 Let's listen! 

STEP 2 Let's practice! CD3 28

STEP 3 Let's chant! 

①

②

③

④

⑤

⑥

⑦

⑧

⑨

⑩

⑪

⑫

Listening Activity

会話を聞いて，時計に時刻の数字を書こう。

CD3 30

①

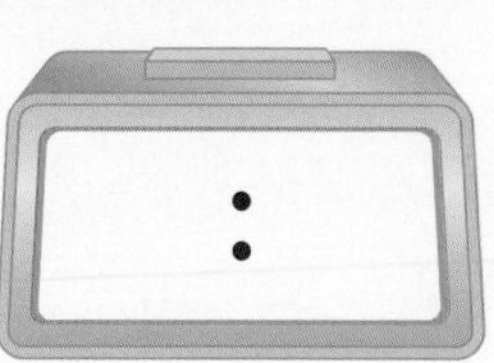

②

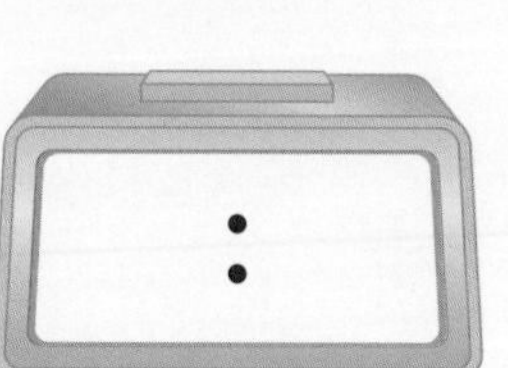

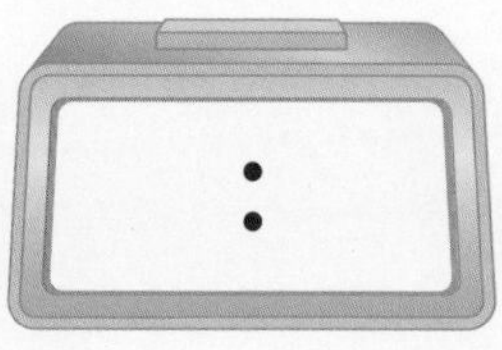

④

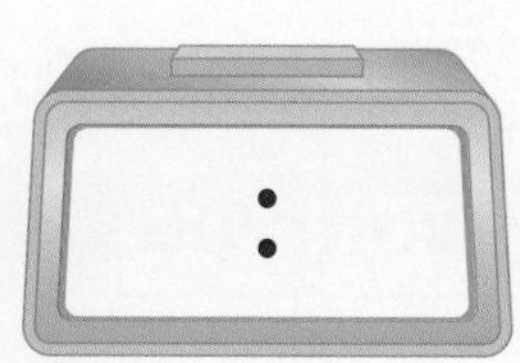

Song 英語の歌を聞いて，歌ってみよう！

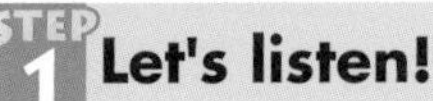 STEP 1 Let's listen!  CD3 31
STEP 2 Let's practice!  CD3 32
STEP 3 Let's sing!  CD3 33

ONE, TWO, BUCKLE MY SHOE

ONE, TWO,
BUCKLE MY SHOE;

THREE, FOUR,
SHUT THE DOOR;

FIVE, SIX,
PICK UP STICKS;

SEVEN, EIGHT,
LAY THEM STRAIGHT;

NINE, TEN,
A BIG FAT HEN.

Learn Some More 対になる言葉を聞いてみよう！

STEP 1 Let's listen! CD3 34　STEP 2 Let's practice! CD3 35

① heavy　② light

Listen to Your Teacher 英語を聞いて，言われた動作をしてみよう！

STEP 1 Let's listen! CD3 36　STEP 2 Let's practice! CD3 37

① 

Listen up.

② 

Speak up, please.

③ 

Please be quiet.

④ 

Listen carefully.

Alphabet Activity

アルファベットソングを歌おう。
英語を聞いて，大文字をグループ分けしよう。

STEP 1 Let's sing! CD3 38

STEP 2 Let's practice! CD3 39

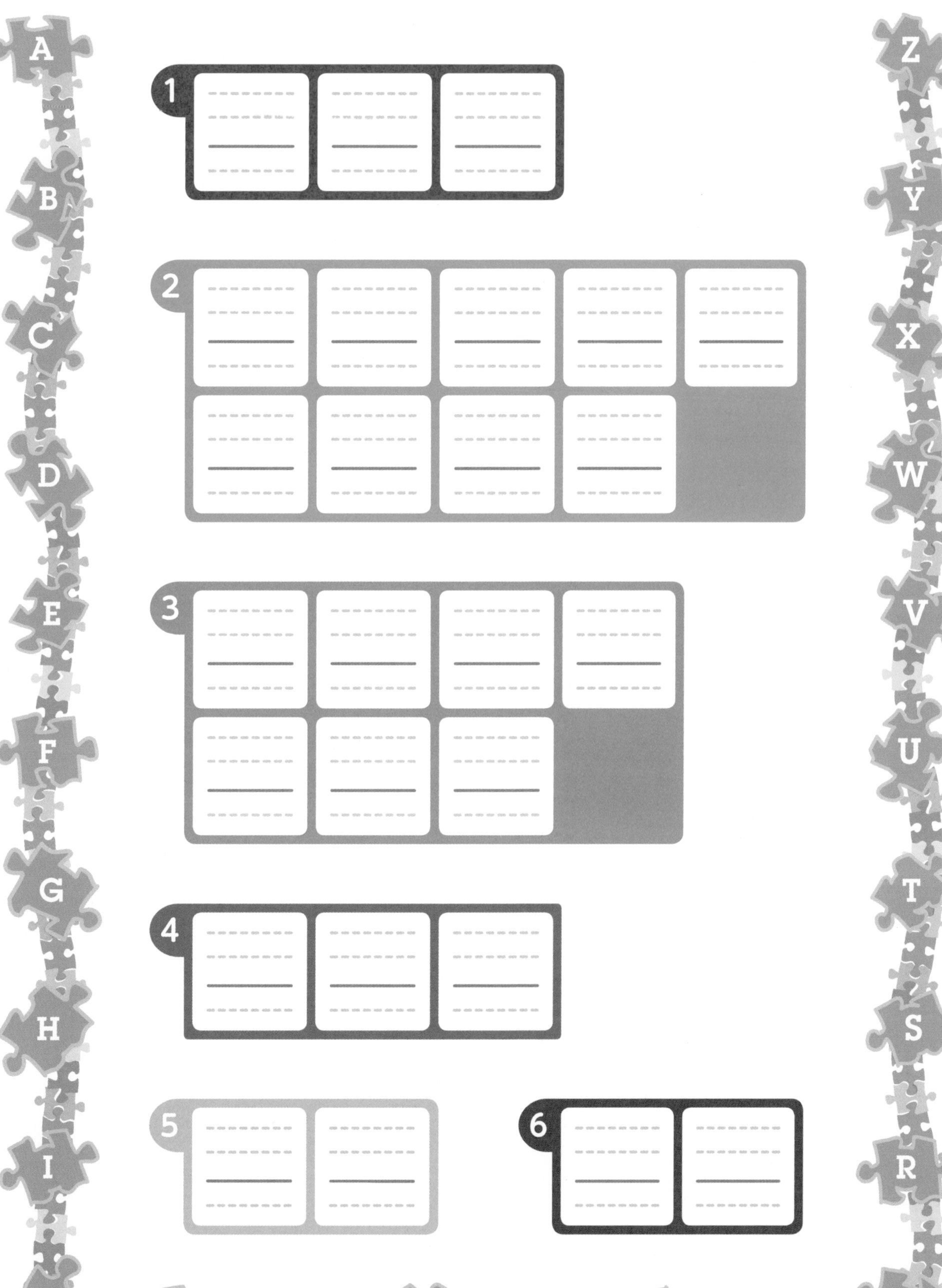

Review 2 Unit 4-6

1 (1)と(2)の対話を聞いて，答えの文の内容にあうイラストに○をつけましょう。

(1)

Yes, I do.

I like   .

(2)

No, I don't.

I don't like   .

2 (1)と(2)の対話を聞いて，答えの文の内容にあうイラストに○をつけましょう。

(1)  What fruit do you like?

 I like 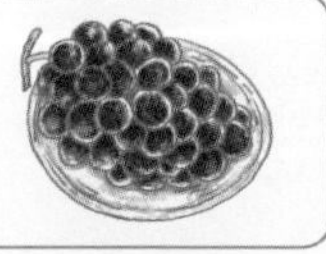 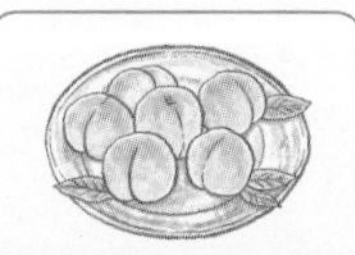  .

How about you, Shohei?

 I like    .

---

(2) What time is it, Hasan?

 It's 

.

3 (1)～(4)の会話を聞いて，内容にあうイラストを下からえらんで，A から D の記号を□に書きましょう。

4 英語を聞いて，内容にあうイラストの□に✓をつけましょう。

(1)

(2)

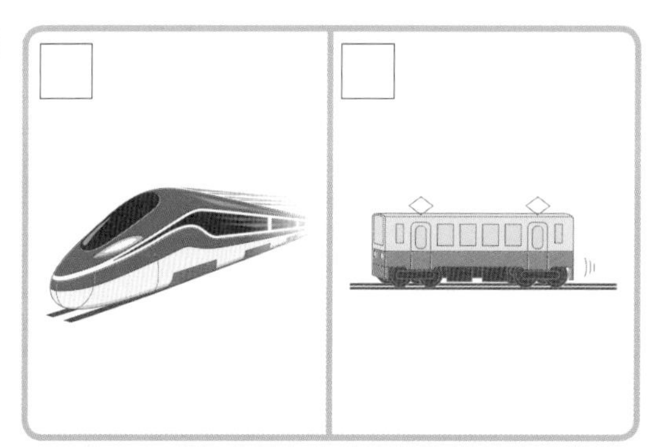

(3)

(4)

Unit 7

- 様々なグリーティングカードの名称に慣れ親しみ，カードを渡すやりとりをする
- いろいろな図形の言い方と，ほしい図形をやりとりする表現に慣れ親しむ

This is for you.

Key Words

特別(とくべつ)な日におくりあうグリーティングカードの名前をおぼえよう！

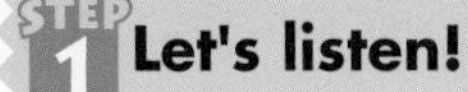

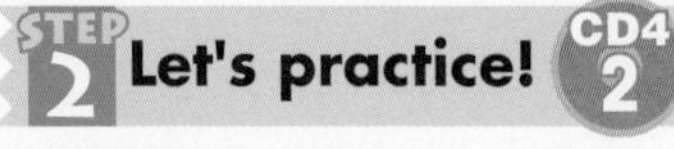

① 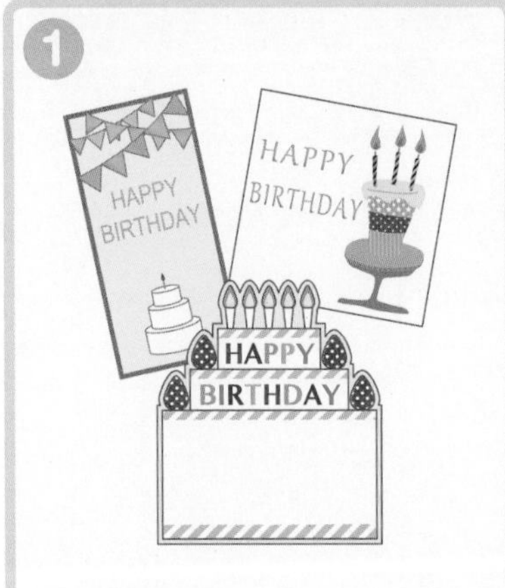

BIRTHDAY CARDS

② 

GET WELL CARDS

③ THANK YOU CARDS

④ 

CHRISTMAS CARDS

⑤ 

NEW YEAR'S CARDS

⑥ 

VALENTINE'S DAY CARDS

⑦ 

MOTHER'S DAY CARDS

⑧ 

FATHER'S DAY CARDS

⑨ 

HALLOWEEN CARDS

カードをおくる場面の会話を聞いてみよう！

STEP 1 Let's listen!  STEP 2 Let's practice!  STEP 3 Let's chant! 

1

Happy Valentine's Day!
This is for you.
HAPPY VALENTINE'S DAY
Dear Mayu,
You are my best friend.
Thank you always.
Anna
Thank you.

2

Kenta is sick in bed.
Let's write the get-well cards for him.
That's a good idea.
Dear Kenta,
GET WELL SOON!
Shohei
Dear Kenta,
GET WELL SOON!
Hasan

Role-play 44ページのイラストを見ながらカードをおくったりもらったりするときの会話をしてみよう。

 Happy [birthday]! / [Get well soon].
This is for you.

 Thank you.

More Words

いろいろな図形の言い方をおぼえよう！

STEP 1 Let's listen! 

STEP 2 Let's practice! 

STEP 3 Let's chant! 

① 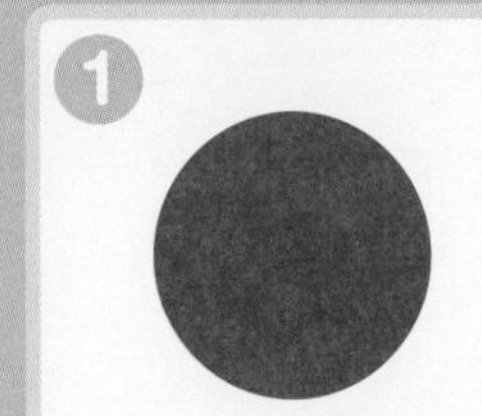
a circle

② 
a triangle

③ 
a square

④ 
a rectangle

⑤ 
a diamond

⑥ 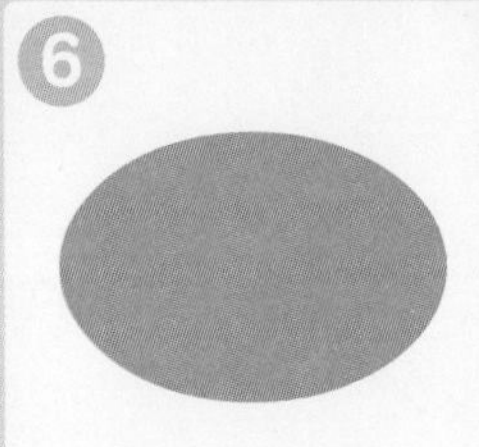
an oval

⑦ 
a star

⑧ 
a heart

Listening Activity

ほしい図形をやりとりする会話を聞いて，
それぞれが作った作品（さくひん）と線でむすぼう。

①  ● ● 

②  ● ● 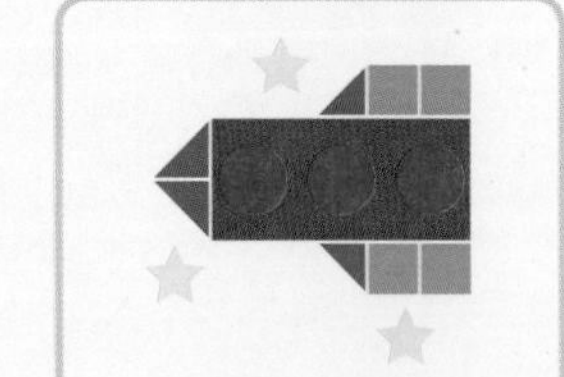

③  ● ● 

④  ● ● 

CORE English

小学 3 年

解答集

WB・A

Unit 1 の答え

テキスト

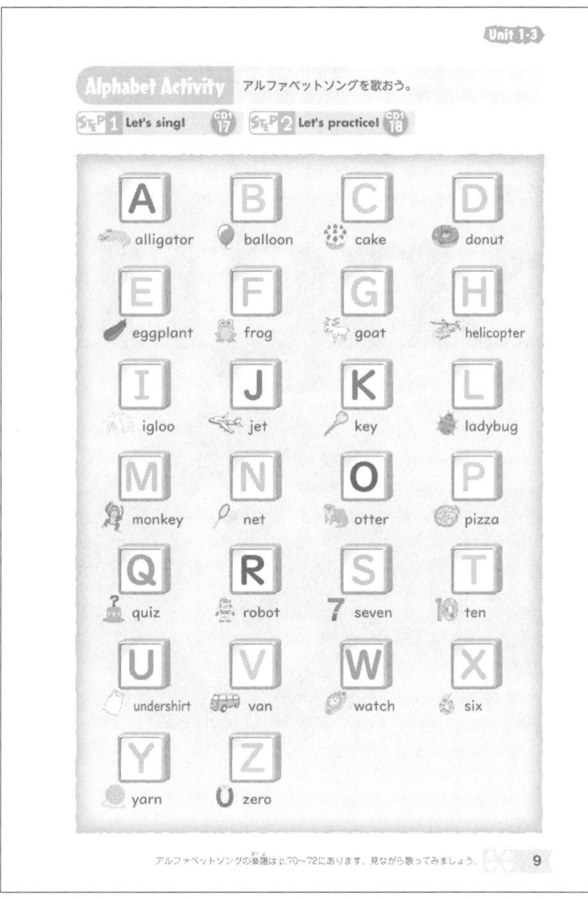

ワークブック

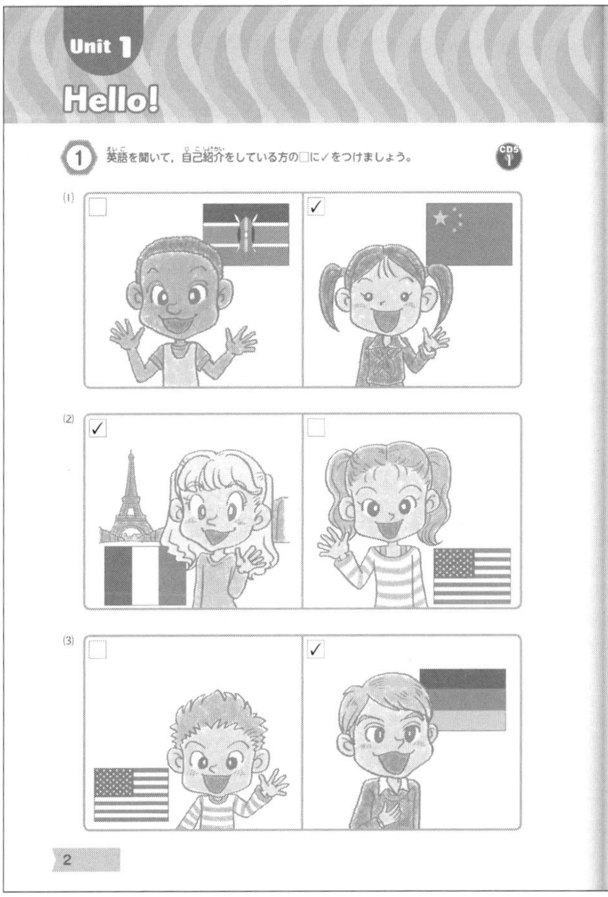

Unit 1

Hello!

① 英語を聞いて，自己紹介をしている方の□に✓をつけましょう。 CD5 1

(1) □ ✓

(2) ✓ □

(3) □ ✓

2

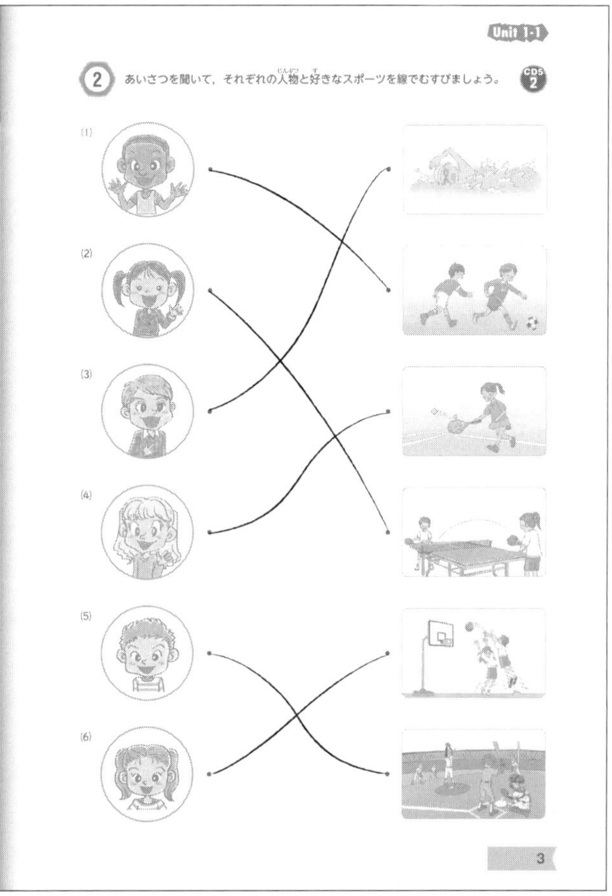

Unit 1-1

② あいさつを聞いて，それぞれの人物と好きなスポーツを線でむすびましょう。 CD5 2

(1)

(2)

(3)

(4)

(5)

(6)

3

ワークブック

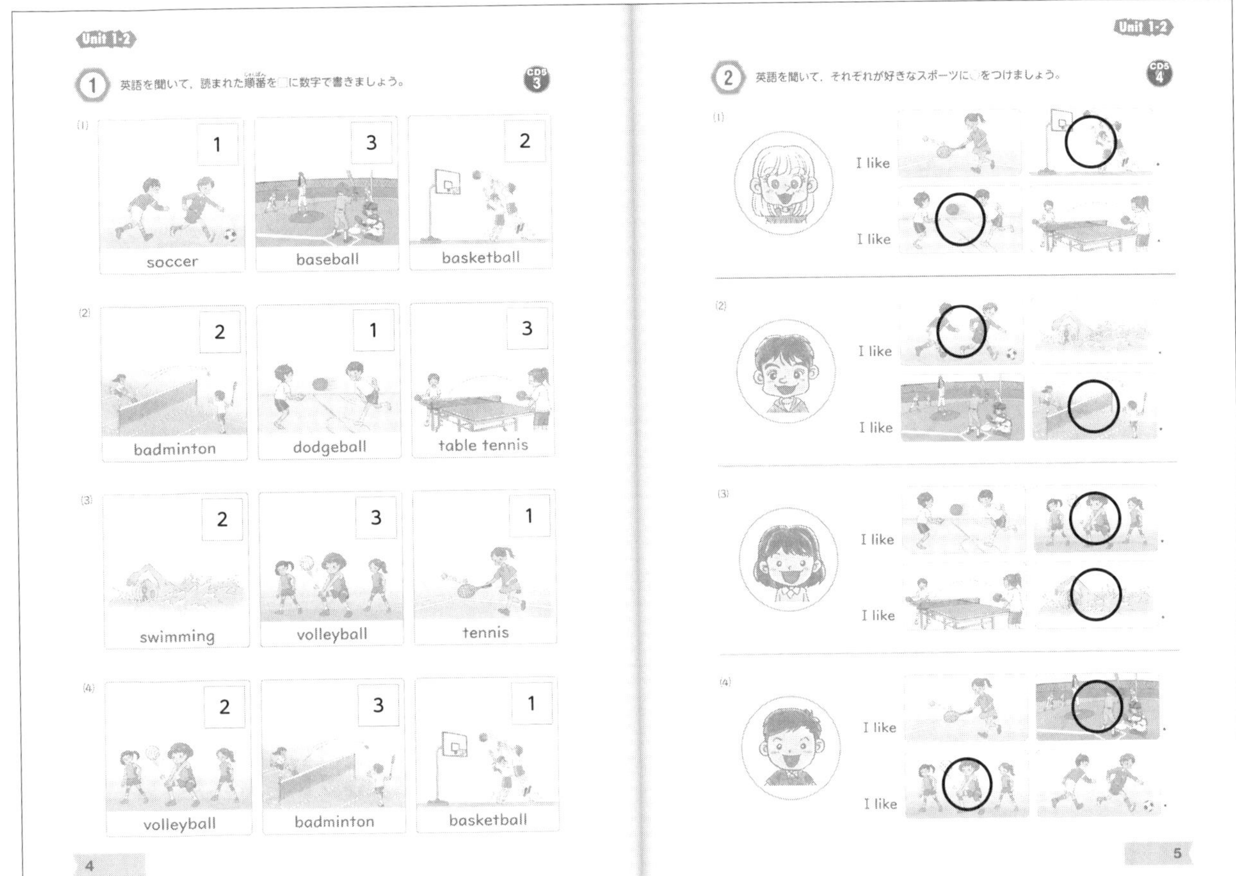

ワークブック

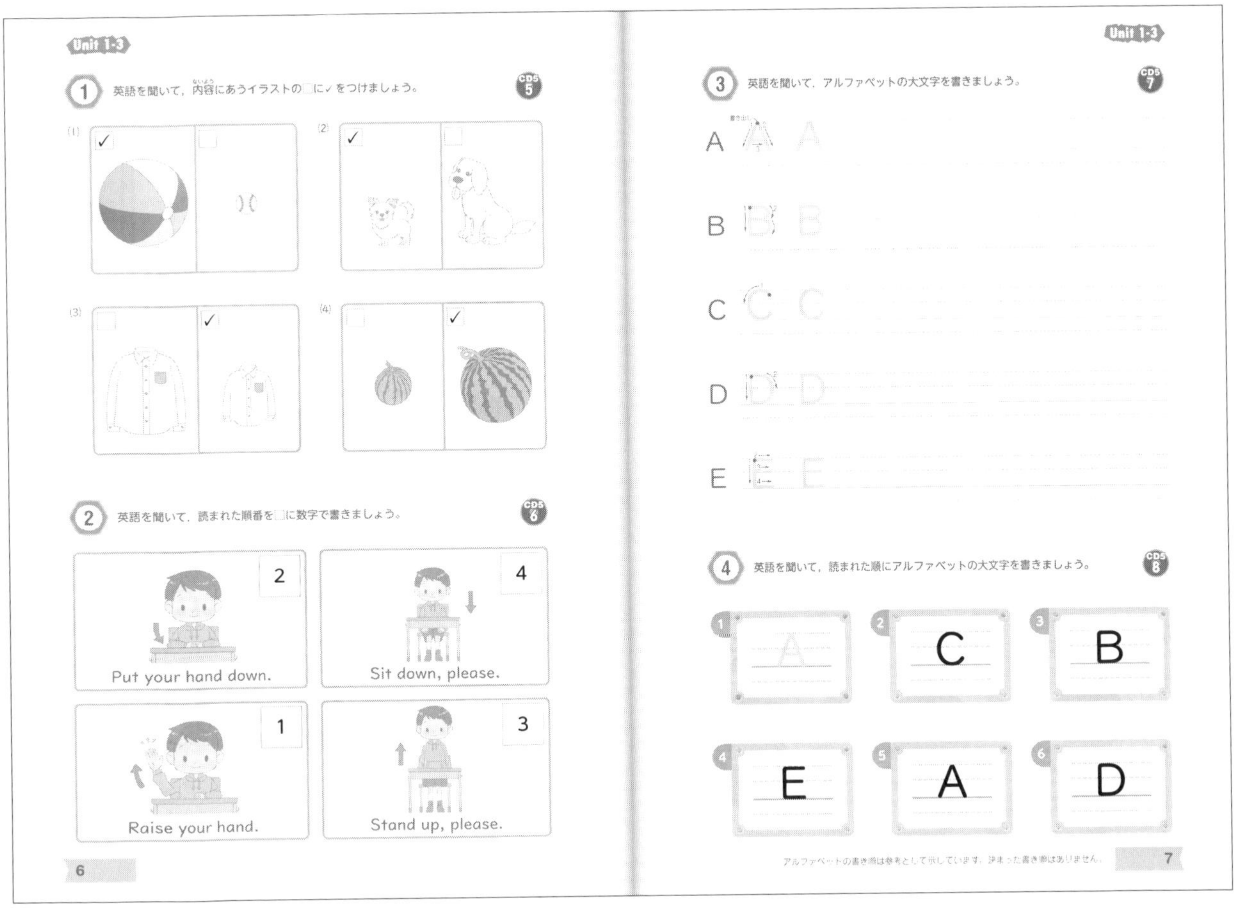

Unit 1-3

1 英語を聞いて，内容にあうイラストの□に✓をつけましょう。

(1) ✓ □
(2) ✓ □
(3) □ ✓
(4) □ ✓

2 英語を聞いて，読まれた順番を□に数字で書きましょう。

2 Put your hand down.	4 Sit down, please.
1 Raise your hand.	3 Stand up, please.

Unit 1-3

3 英語を聞いて，アルファベットの大文字を書きましょう。

A A A
B B B
C C C
D D D
E E E

4 英語を聞いて，読まれた順にアルファベットの大文字を書きましょう。

1 A　2 C　3 B
4 E　5 A　6 D

アルファベットの書き順は参考として示しています。決まった書き順はありません。

Song 英語の歌を聞いて，歌ってみよう！

STEP 1 Let's listen!  STEP 2 Let's practice!  STEP 3 Let's sing! 

This Is For You

HAPPY HALLOWEEN, HAPPY HOLIDAYS,

HAPPY NEW YEAR.

HAPPY MOTHER'S DAY, HAPPY FATHER'S DAY,

HAPPY BIRTHDAY.

HAPPY VALENTINE'S DAY.

GET WELL SOON.

THANK YOU, MY FRIEND.

THIS IS FOR YOU.

Learn Some More

対になる言葉を聞いてみよう！

STEP 1 Let's listen! CD4 14

STEP 2 Let's practice! CD4 15

①

strong

②

weak

Listen to Your Teacher

英語を聞いて，言われた動作をしてみよう！

STEP 1 Let's listen! 

STEP 2 Let's practice! 

①

Hold hands.

②

Let go of your hands.

③

Make a circle.

④

Make pairs.

Alphabet Activity

アルファベットソングを歌おう。
英語を聞いて，A～Z までの順番で大文字を書いてみよう。

STEP 1 Let's sing! CD4 18

STEP 2 Let's practice! CD4 19

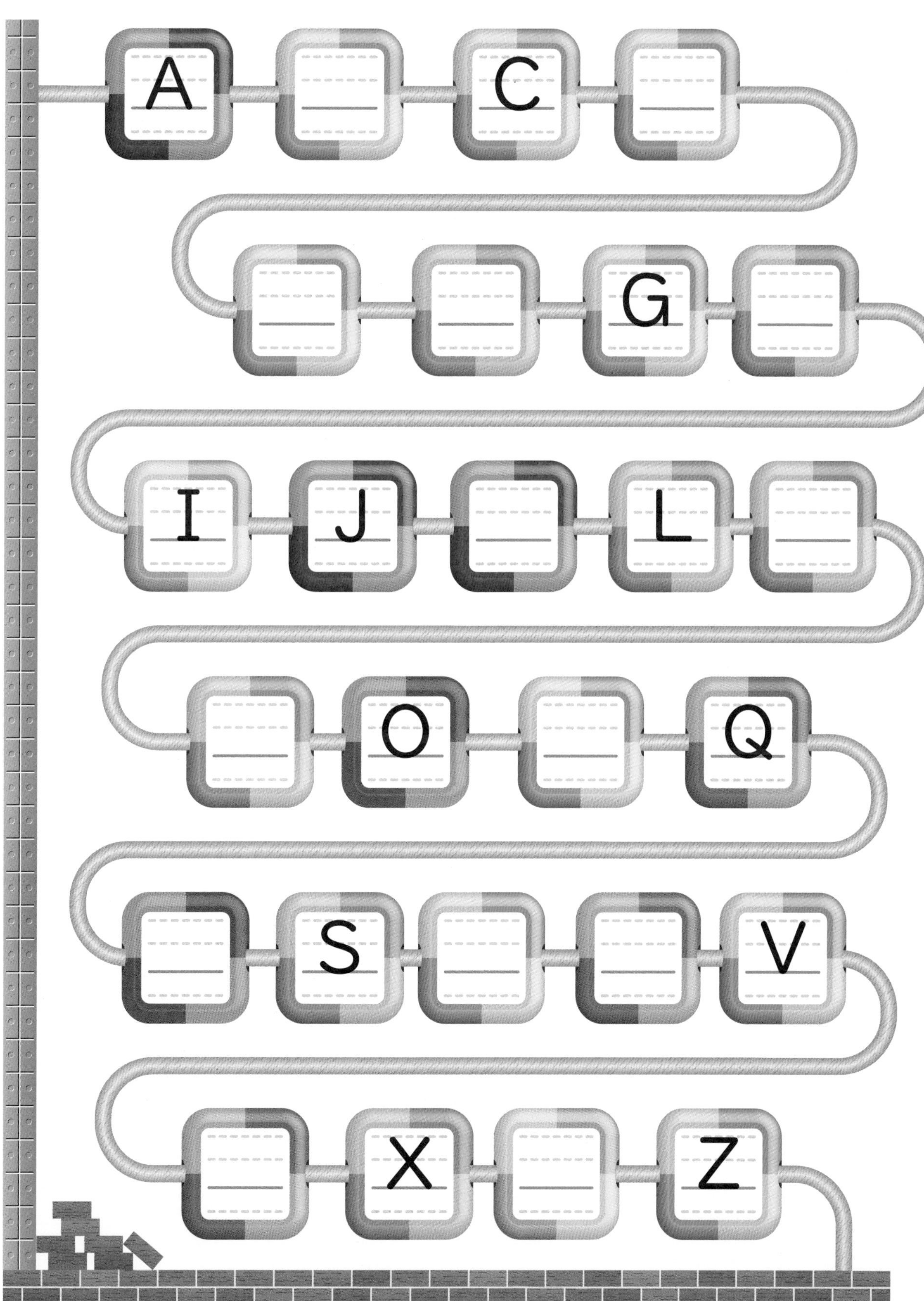

Unit 8 □体の部分の言い方に慣れ親しみ，それぞれの部分の名称をたずねたり答えたりする
□十二支の動物の言い方と，干支当てスリーヒントクイズに慣れ親しむ

What's this?

Key Words ロボットの組み立て図を見て，体の部分の言い方をおぼえよう！

STEP 1 Let's listen! CD4 20

STEP 2 Let's practice! CD4 21

STEP 3 Let's chant! CD4 22

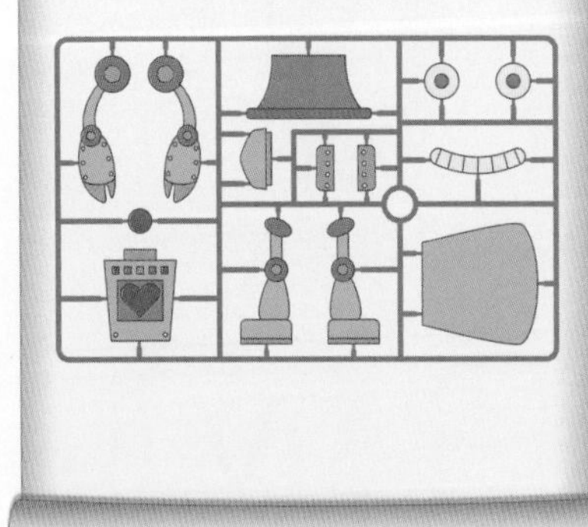

① eyes

② ears

③ nose

④ mouth

⑤ face

⑥ head

⑦ neck

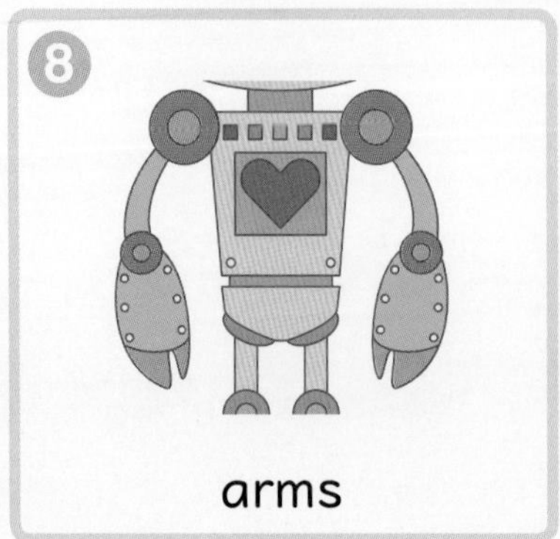

⑧ arms

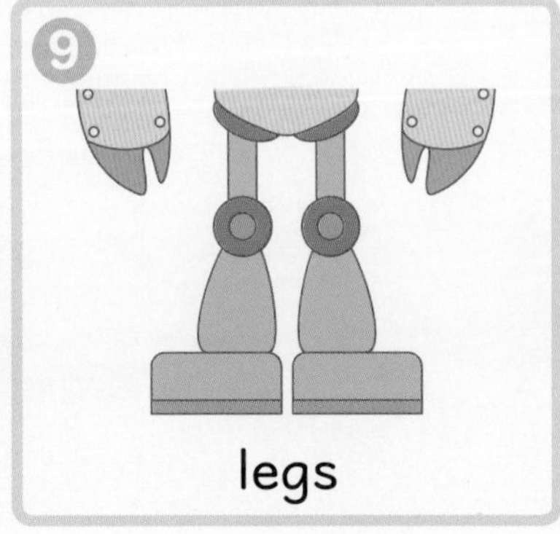

⑨ legs

Listen and Talk　体の部分についての会話を聞いてみよう！

STEP 1 Let's listen! CD4 23　STEP 2 Let's practice! CD4 24　STEP 3 Let's chant! CD4 25

1

2

Role-play 自分の体の部分を指して，英語の言い方をたずねてみよう。

What's this? / What are these?

It's a [head]. / They're [arms].

More Words
干支（えと）の動物（どうぶつ）の言い方をおぼえよう！

STEP 1 Let's listen! CD4 26　STEP 2 Let's practice! CD4 27　STEP 3 Let's chant! CD4 28

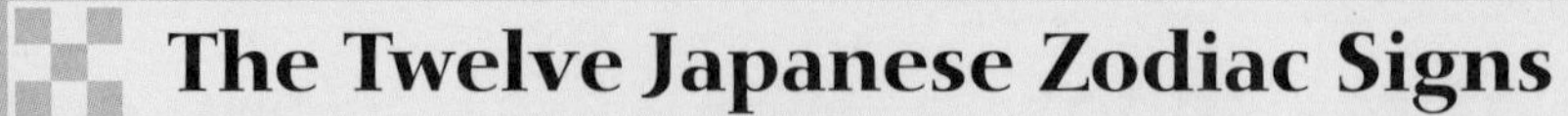

The Twelve Japanese Zodiac Signs

① 

the mouse

② 

the ox

③ 

the tiger

④ 

the rabbit

⑤ 

the dragon

⑥ 

the snake

⑦ 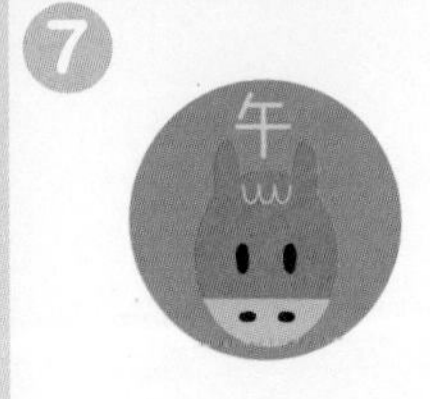

the horse

⑧ 

the sheep

⑨ 

the monkey

⑩ 

the rooster

⑪ 

the dog

⑫ 

the wild boar

Listening Activity
それぞれの干支を聞いて，上のイラストの番号を書こう。

CD4 29

①  

②  

③  

④  

Song 英語の歌を聞いて，歌ってみよう！

STEP 1 Let's listen! CD4 30　STEP 2 Let's practice! CD4 31　STEP 3 Let's sing! CD4 32

The Body Parts Song

Pat your head,
Rub your face,
Touch your neck,
Cross your arms,
Touch your shoulders,
Touch your knees.
Let's have fun together!
Cover your eyes,
Touch your ears,
Point to your nose,
Cover your mouth,
Stomp your feet,
Clap your hands.
Let's have fun together!

Learn Some More

対になる言葉を聞いてみよう！

STEP 1 Let's listen! CD4 33　STEP 2 Let's practice! CD4 34

①

long

②

short

Listen to Your Teacher

英語を聞いて，言われた動作をしてみよう！

STEP 1 Let's listen! CD4 35　STEP 2 Let's practice! CD4 36

①

Make a line.

②

Make two lines.

③

Face each other.

④

Ask each other.

Alphabet Activity

アルファベットソングを歌おう。
アルファベット順にならべて書こう。

書きおわったら，STEP2 の音声を聞いて答え合わせをしよう。

1 

2 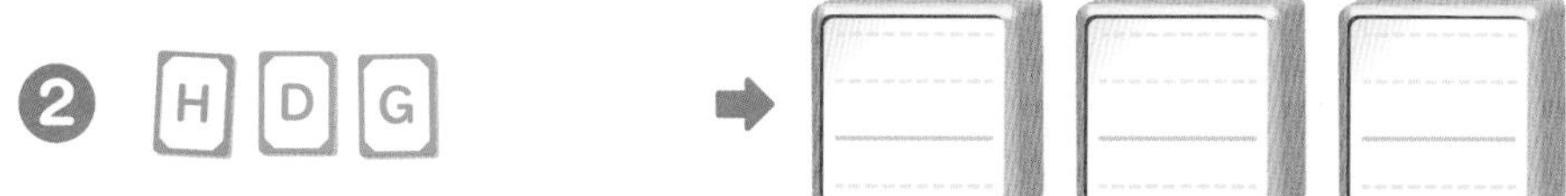

3 

4 

5 

6 

7 F O H E G J

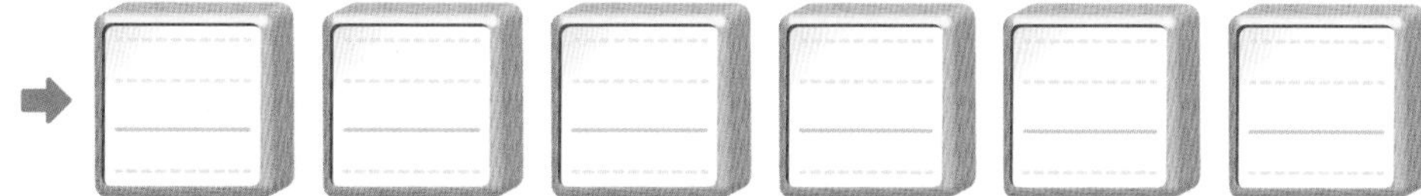

8 M T A E W R

Unit 9

□絵本のような短い話を聞いて，おおよその内容がわかる
□小動物や海の生き物の言い方と，動物当てクイズに慣れ親しむ

Who are you?

Listen and Talk

絵本のページを見ながら英語を聞いて，
話の内容をつかもう！

STEP 1 Let's listen! CD4 39　STEP 2 Let's practice! CD4 40　STEP 3 Let's chant! CD4 41

Who are you?

I see something long and shiny.
Who are you?
Are you a snake?

Yes, I am.
I'm a snake.

1

I see something white and furry.
Who are you?
Are you a sheep?

Yes, I am.
I'm a sheep.

2

I see something long and white.
Who are you?
Are you a rabbit?

Yes, I am.
I'm a rabbit.

3

I see something little and gray.
Who are you?
Are you a mouse?

Yes, I am.
I'm a mouse.

4

I see something tall and red.
Who are you?
Are you a rooster?

Yes, I am.
I'm a rooster.

5

More Words

動物の言い方をおぼえよう！

STEP 1 Let's listen! CD4 42
STEP 2 Let's practice! CD4 43
STEP 3 Let's chant! CD4 44

1

a cat

2

a whale

3

a turtle

4

a lizard

5

a squirrel

6

a pig

Listening Activity

写真を見ながら英語を聞いて，
どの動物か上のイラストの番号を書こう。

1
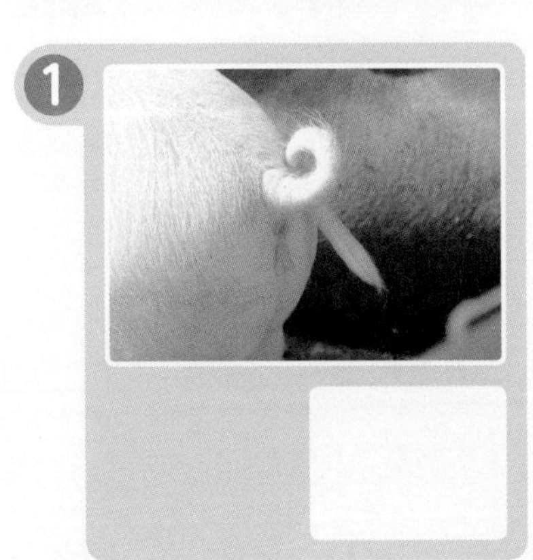

2

3

4

5

6
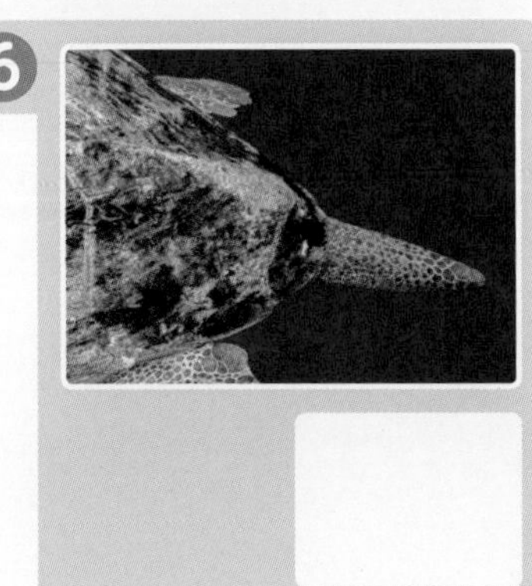

Song 英語の歌を聞いて，歌ってみよう！

STEP 1 Let's listen! CD4 46　STEP 2 Let's practice! CD4 47　STEP 3 Let's sing! CD4 48

Who Are You?

I see something long and shiny.
Who are you? Are you a snake?
Yes, I am. I'm a snake. Hiss, hiss, hiss.

I see something white and furry.
Who are you? Are you a sheep?
Yes, I am. I'm a sheep. Baa, baa, baa.

I see something long and white.
Who are you? Are you a rabbit?
Yes, I am. I'm a rabbit. Hop, hop, hop.

I see something little and gray.
Who are you? Are you a mouse?
Yes, I am. I'm a mouse. Squeak, squeak, squeak.

I see something tall and red.
Who are you? Are you a rooster?
Yes, I am. I'm a rooster. Cock-a-doodle-doo.

Learn Some More

対になる言葉を聞いてみよう！

STEP 1 Let's listen! CD4 49

STEP 2 Let's practice! CD4 50

① 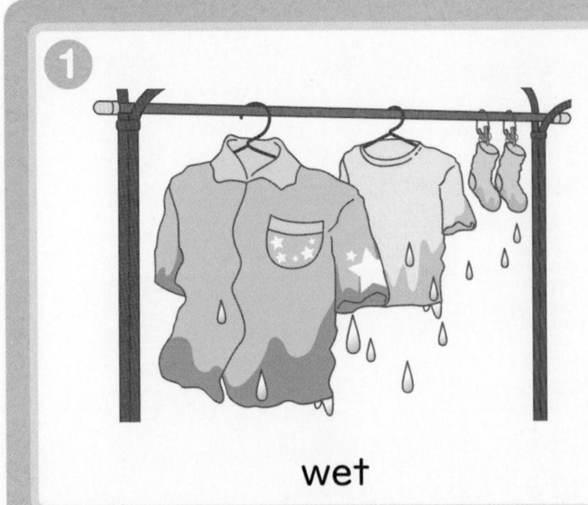

wet

② 

dry

Listen to Your Teacher

英語を聞いて，言われた動作をしてみよう！

STEP 1 Let's listen! CD4 51

STEP 2 Let's practice! CD4 52

① 

Take a step forward.

② 

Take a step back.

③ 

Take a step to the right.

④ 

Take a step to the left.

Alphabet Activity

アルファベットソングを歌おう。
アルファベット順になるように，前後の大文字を書こう。

書きおわったら，STEP2 の音声を聞いて答え合わせをしよう。

17
S

Review 3 Unit 7-9

1 (1)～(3)の対話を聞いて，答えの文の内容にあうイラストに○をつけましょう。

(1)

 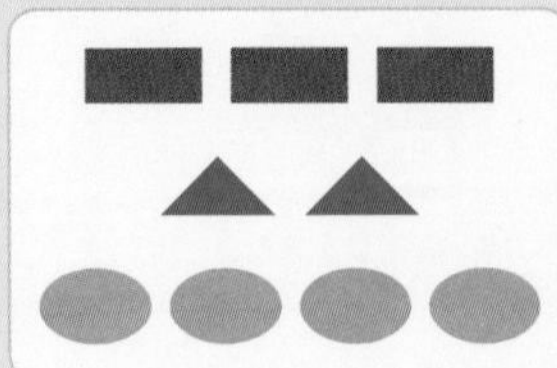 , please.

(2)

It's a   .

(3)

They're  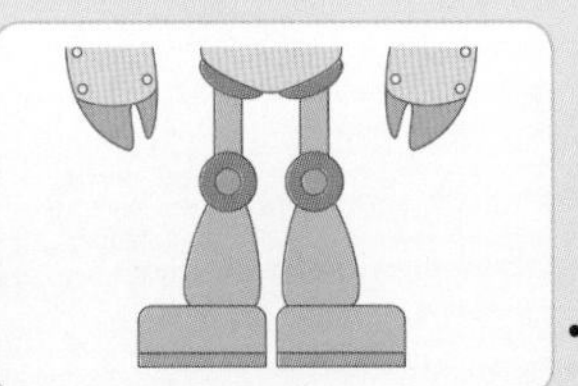 .

2 対話を聞いて，内容にあうイラストに○をつけましょう。

Who are you?

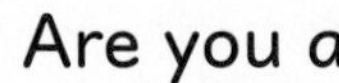    ?

Are you a

No, I'm not.

I'm a    .

3 (1)～(4)の会話を聞いて，内容にあうイラストを下からえらんで，A から D の記号を□に書きましょう。

CD4
57

(1) □　(2) □　(3) □　(4) □

A
HAPPY VALENTINE'S DAY
Dear Mayu,
You are my best friend.
Thank you always.
Anna

B

C

D
Dear Kenta,
GET WELL SOON!
Shohei
Dear Kenta,
GET WELL SOON!
Hasan

4 英語を聞いて，あっている方の□に✓をつけましょう。

CD4
58

(1)

(2)

(3)

(4)

単元別 Word List

Unit 1

74 words

about
alligator
America
and
badminton
balloon
baseball
basketball
big
cake
China
day
do
dodgeball
donut
down
eggplant
France
frog
Germany
goat
hand
helicopter
hello
hi
how
I
igloo
I'm (=I am)
in
international
is
jet
Kenya
key
ladybug
like
live
meet
monkey
my
name
net
nice
otter
pizza
please
put
quiz
raise
robot
seven
sit
six
small
soccer
sport
stand
swimming
table tennis
ten
tennis
to
undershirt
up
van
volleyball
watch
we
what
yarn
you
your
zero

Unit 2 (32 words)

are

away

cereal

cheese

fine

good

great

happy

hungry

jam

milk

morning

not

orange juice

out

pencil

pick

pudding

sad

salad

sleepy

so

take

textbook

thank

thirsty

tired

toast

today

very

yucky

yummy

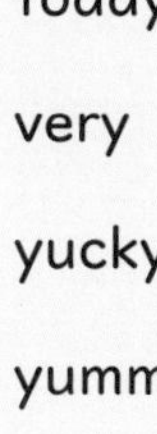

Unit 3 (56 words)

a

again

alive

because

bit (← bite)

bite

caught (← catch)

close

crayons (← crayon)

dice

did

eight

eighteen

eleven

erasers (← eraser)

fifteen

finger

fish

five

four

fourteen

give

go

it

job

let

little

many

marbles (← marble)
me
minus
nine
nineteen
oh
on
once
one
open
plus
right
rulers (← ruler)
seventeen
sixteen
that's (= that is)
the
then
thirteen
this
three
try
twelve
twenty
two
which
why
wrong

Unit 4 38 words

black
blue
brown
carrots (← carrot)
color
colors (← color)
cucumbers (← cucumber)
don't (= do not)
draw
green peppers
(← green pepper)
jeans
letters (← letter)
look
lots (← lot)
mushrooms
(← mushroom)
new
no
of
old
onions (← onion)
orange
pants
picture
pink
pretty
pumpkins (← pumpkin)
purple
red
shirt
sweet potatoes
(← sweet potato)
tomatoes (← tomato)
too
trace
white
wow
write
yellow
yes

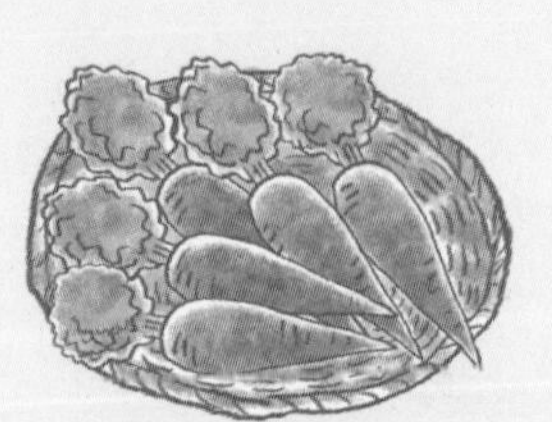

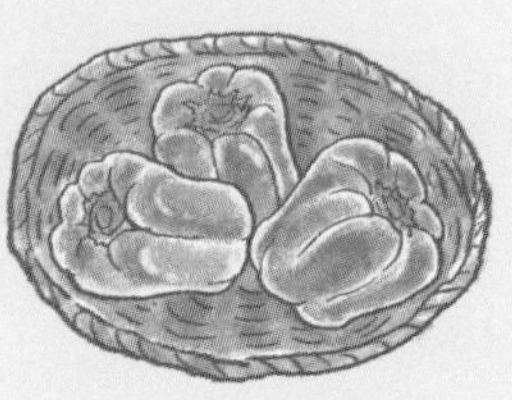

Unit 5 26 words

apples (← apple)
at
bananas (← banana)
bread
cherries (← cherry)
chocolate
fast
food
fried chicken
fruit
grapes (← grape)
hamburgers
(← hamburger)
ice cream
letter
noodles (← noodle)
peaches (← peach)
pears (← pear)
persimmons (← persimmon)
point
rice
sandwiches (← sandwich)
show
slow
spaghetti
strawberries
(← strawberry)
touch

Unit 6 35 words

alphabet
be
buckle
can
carefully
chart
door
fat
fifty-eight (58)
fifty-four (54)
fifty-nine (59)
fifty-seven (57)
forty-five (45)
forty-two (42)
heavy
hen
lay
light
listen
number
numbers (← number)
quiet
see
shoe
shut
speak
sticks (← stick)
straight
them
thirty-six (36)
thirty-three (33)
time
twenty-eight (28)
twenty-four (24)
twenty-one (21)

Unit 7 (33 words)

an
bed
birthday
cards (← card)
Christmas
circle
diamond
Father's Day
for
friend
get
Halloween
heart
him
hold
holidays (← holiday)
idea
let's
make
Mother's Day
New Year
oval
pairs (← pair)
rectangle
sick
soon
square
star
strong
triangle
Valentine's Day
weak
well

Unit 8 (50 words)

arms (← arm)
ask
body
clap
cover
cross
cute
dog
dragon
each
ears (← ear)
eyes (← eye)
face
feet (← foot)
fun
have
head
horse
it's (= it is)
Japanese
knees (← knee)
legs (← leg)
line
long
mouse
mouth
neck
nose

other

ox

parts (← part)

pat

rabbit

rooster

rub

sheep

short

shoulders (← shoulder)

signs (← sign)

snake

song

stomp

tail

these

they're (= they are)

tiger

together

what's (= what is)

wild boar

zodiac

Unit 9 24 words

am

baa

back

cat

cock-a-doodle-doo

dry

forward

furry

gray

hiss

hop

left

lizard

pig

shiny

something

squeak

squirrel

step

tall

turtle

wet

whale

who

Alphabet Songs

Unit1～9の Alphabet Activity に入っているアルファベットソングの楽譜です。
これを見ながら歌ってみましょう。

Aa Bb Cc Dd Ee Ff Gg Hh Ii
Jj Kk Ll Mm Nn Oo Pp Qq Rr
Ss Tt Uu Vv Ww Xx Yy Zz

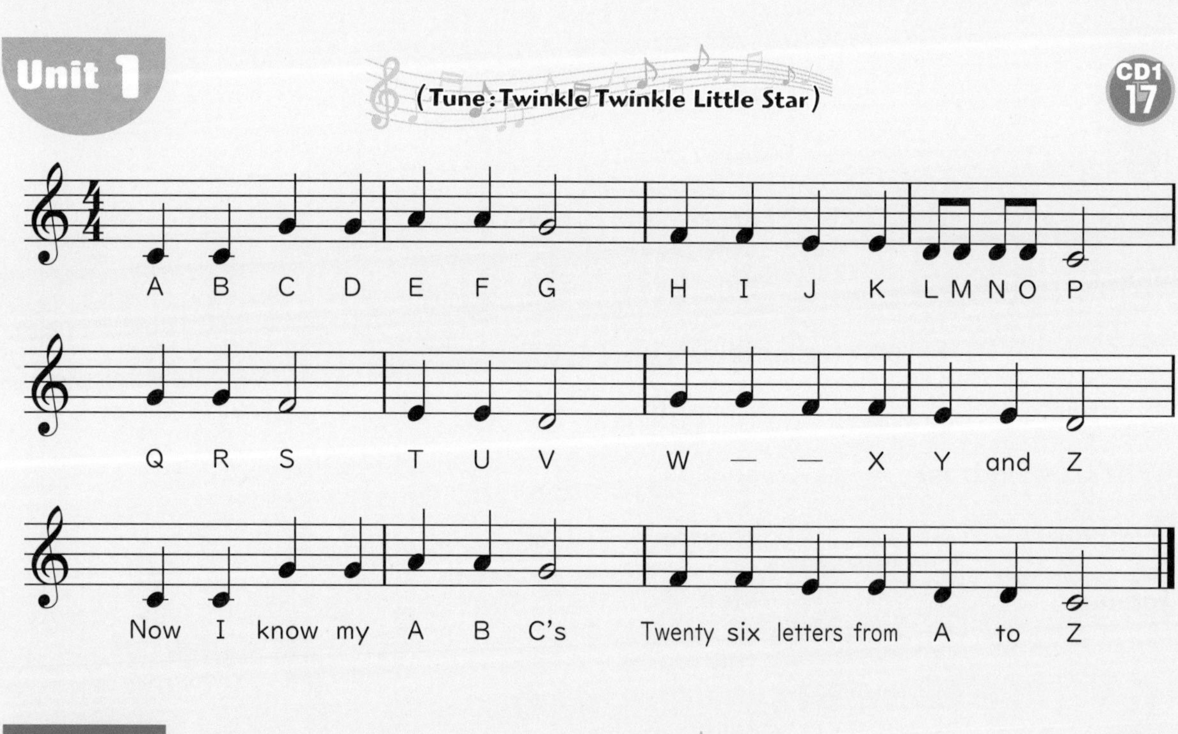

Unit 1
(Tune : Twinkle Twinkle Little Star)
CD1 17
A B C D E F G H I J K L M N O P
Q R S T U V W — — X Y and Z
Now I know my A B C's Twenty six letters from A to Z

Unit 3
(Tune: London Bridge ver.2)
CD2 18
A B C D E F G H I J K L M
N O P Q R S T U V W — X Y Z
Unit 4
(Tune: Mary Had a Little Lamb)
CD2 41
A B C D E F G H I J K L M
N O P Q R S T U V W — X Y Z
Unit 5
(Tune: This Old Man)
CD3 18
A B C D E F G H I J K L M N O
P Q R S T — U V — W — X Y Z
Unit 6
(Tune: Where Is Thumbkin)
CD3 38
A B C D E F G H I J K L M N
O P Q R S T U V W— — X Y and Z Y and Z

Unit 7
(Tune: Head, Shoulders, Knees and Toes)
CD4 18
A B C D E F G H I J K L M N O P Q R S — T
U V W — X — Y — Z sing the Al-pha-bet with me sing with me
Unit 8
(Tune: Row Row Row Your Boat)
CD4 37
A B C D E F G H I J KLMNOPQRSTUV W- - X Y Z
Unit 9
(Tune: Row Row Row Your Boat - Round)
CD4 53
A B C D E F G H I J KLMNOPQRSTUV W- - X Y Z
A B C D E F G H I J KLMNOPQRSTUV
A B C D E F G H I J
W- - X Y Z
KLMNOPQRSTUV W- - X Y Z

CORE English

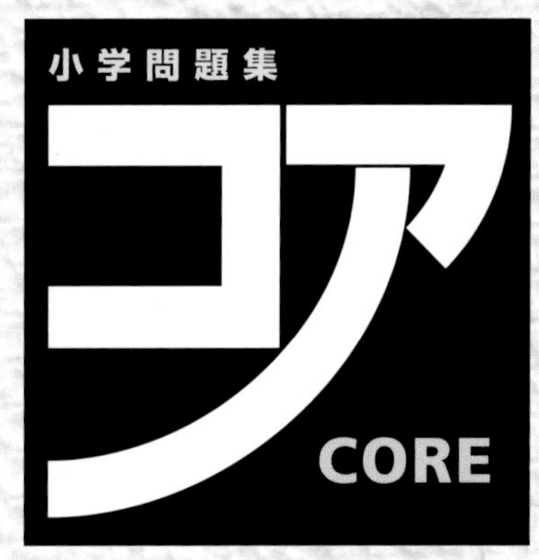

小学 3 年

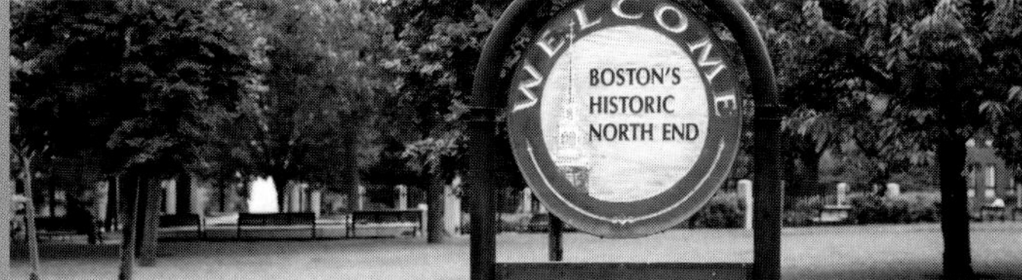

Workbook

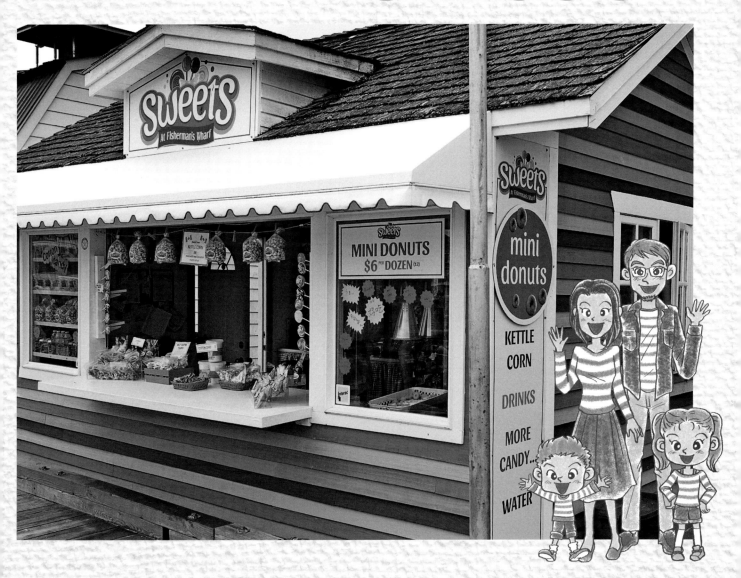

CORE English Workbook

小学3年

もくじ

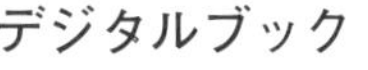

デジタルブック

(タブレットやスマートフォンで読み取ってください。)

＜動作環境＞Google Chrome / Safari (Mac)

インターネットに接続できる環境が必要です。Wi-Fi での使用をオススメします。

Unit 1

Hello!

1 英語を聞いて，自己紹介をしている方の□に✓をつけましょう。

(1)

(2)

(3)

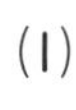

2 あいさつを聞いて，それぞれの人物(じんぶつ)と好(す)きなスポーツを線でむすびましょう。

(1)

(2)

(3)

(4)

(5)

(6)

1 英語を聞いて，読まれた順番を□に数字で書きましょう。

(1)

soccer

baseball

basketball

(2)

badminton

dodgeball

table tennis

(3)

swimming

volleyball

tennis

(4)

volleyball

badminton

basketball

英語を聞いて，それぞれが好きなスポーツに○をつけましょう。

(1)

I like  .

I like  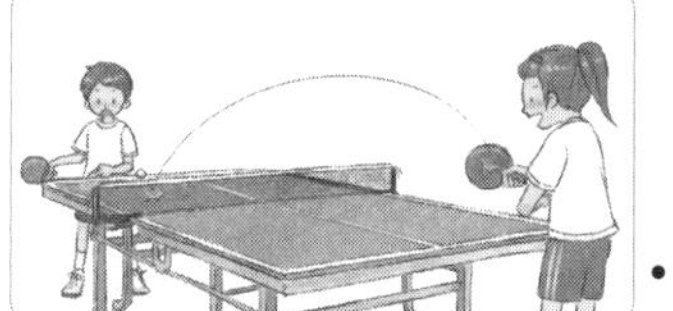 .

(2)

I like  .

I like  .

(3)

I like   .

I like 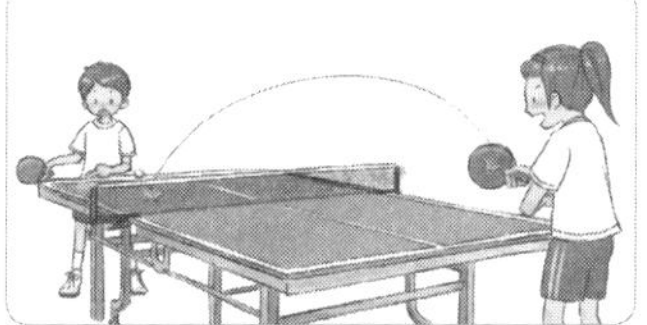  .

(4)

I like   .

I like   .

1 英語を聞いて，内容（ないよう）にあうイラストの□に✓をつけましょう。

(1)

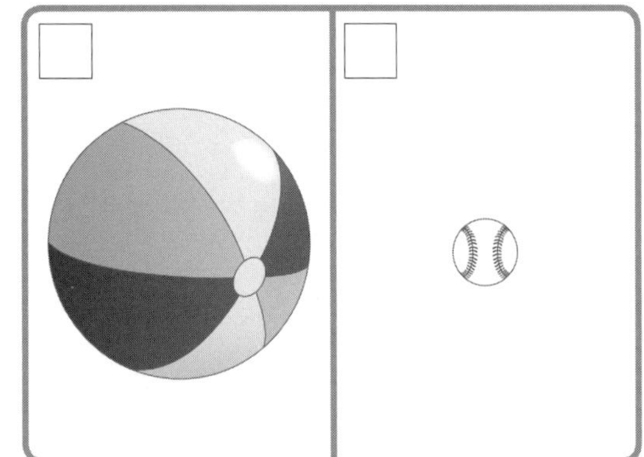

(2)

(3)

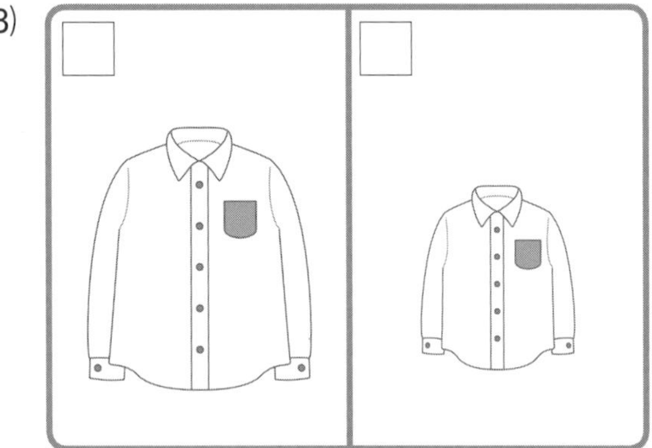

(4)

2 英語を聞いて，読まれた順番を□に数字で書きましょう。

Put your hand down.

Sit down, please.

Raise your hand.

Stand up, please.

3 英語を聞いて，アルファベットの大文字を書きましょう。 CD5 7

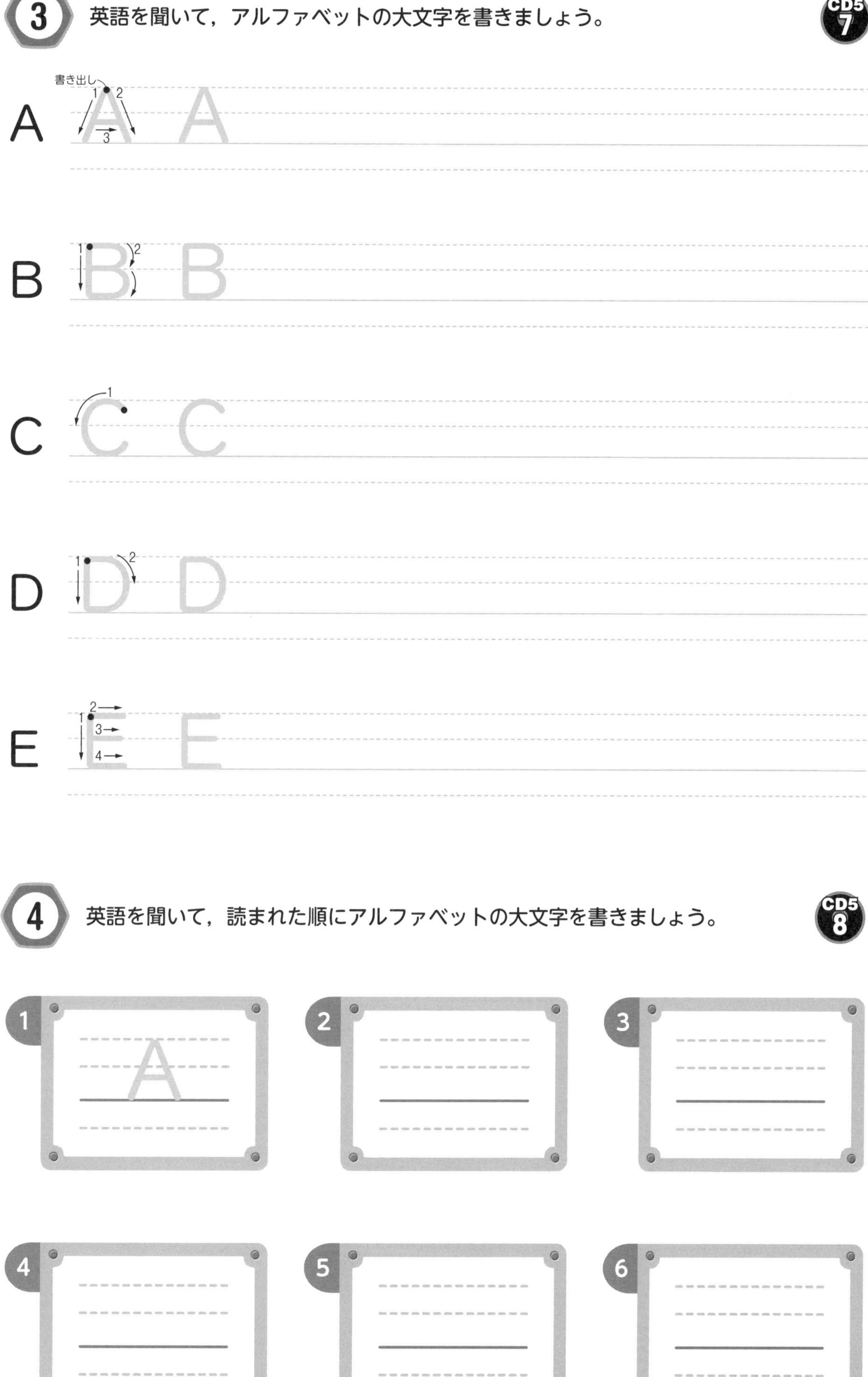

4 英語を聞いて，読まれた順にアルファベットの大文字を書きましょう。 CD5 8

1 A
2
3
4
5
6

アルファベットの書き順は参考として示しています。決まった書き順はありません。

Unit 2

How are you?

英語を聞いて，読まれた順番を□に数字で書きましょう。

(1)

hungry

good

sad

(2)

happy

sleepy

fine

(3)

tired

great

thirsty

対話を聞いて，読まれた気持ちや状態に○をつけましょう。

How are you?

(1)

  .

(2)

I'm   .

(3)

I'm   .

(4)

I'm   .

1 英語を聞いて，読まれた順番を□に数字で書きましょう。

(1)

cereal

milk

toast

(2)

salad

cheese

orange juice

(3)

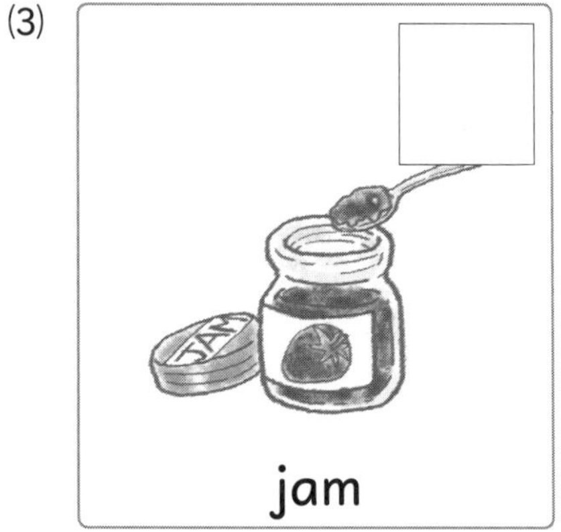

jam

pudding

cake

(4)

cereal

salad

pudding

英語を聞いて，それぞれが好きな食べ物や飲み物に○をつけましょう。

(1)

I like 

.

I like   .

(2)

I like  .

I like 

.

(3)

I like  

.

I like   .

(4)

I like  .

I like 

 .

1 英語を聞いて，読まれた順番を□に数字で書きましょう。

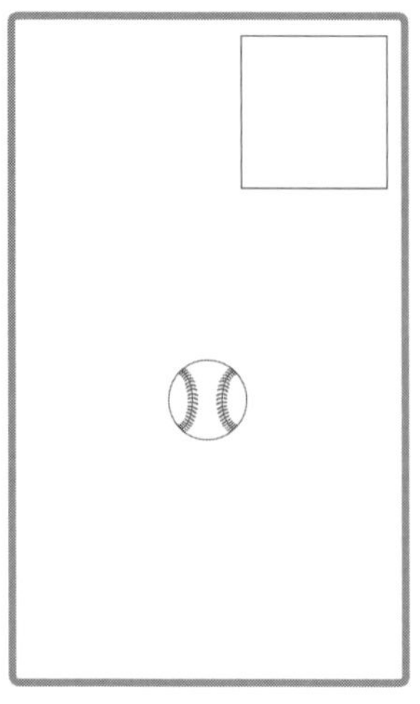

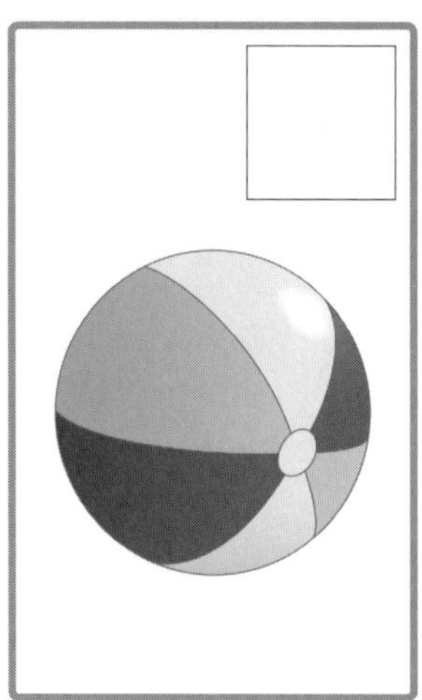

2 英語を聞いて，読まれた順番を□に数字で書きましょう。

Take out your textbook.

Pick up your pencil.

Raise your hand.

Put your textbook away.

Put your hand down.

Put your pencil down.

3 英語を聞いて，アルファベットの大文字を書きましょう。 CD5 15

4 英語を聞いて，読まれた順にアルファベットの大文字を書きましょう。 CD5 16

1
2
3
4
5
6

Unit 3

How many?

英語を聞いて，読まれた数を数字で左から順に丸い枠(わく)の中に書きましょう。

(1)

9			

(2)

(3)

(4)

(5)

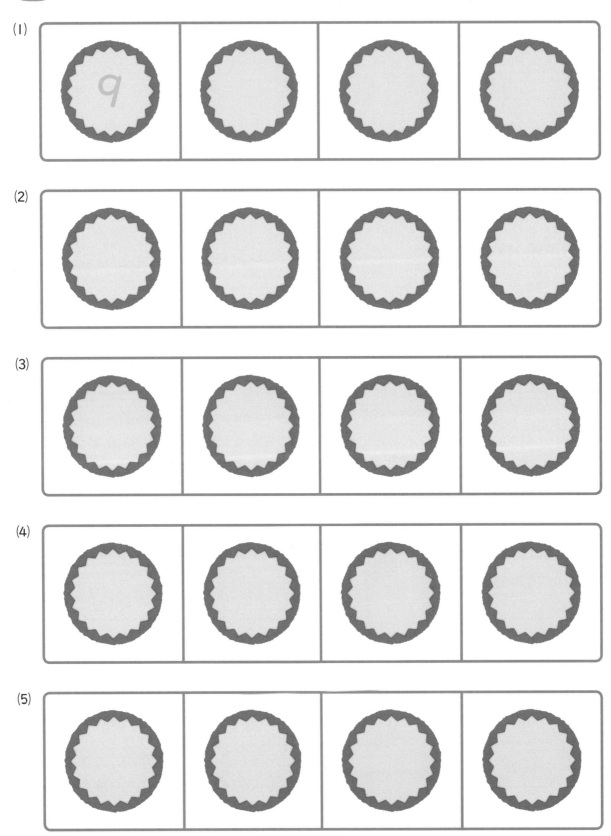

対話を聞いて，読まれた数を□に数字で書きましょう。

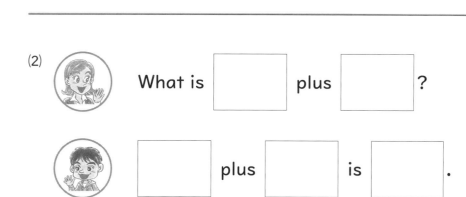

(1)

What is ☐ plus ☐ ?

☐ plus ☐ is ☐ .

---

(2)

What is ☐ plus ☐ ?

☐ plus ☐ is ☐ .

---

(3)

What is ☐ minus ☐ ?

☐ minus ☐ is ☐ .

---

(4)

What is ☐ minus ☐ ?

☐ minus ☐ is ☐ .

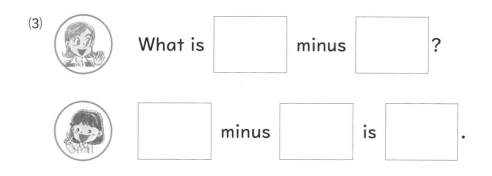

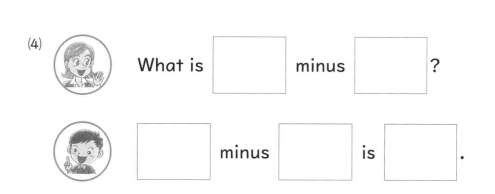

1 対話を聞いて，読まれた文房具（ぶんぼうぐ）に○をつけましょう。

(1)

How many rulers?

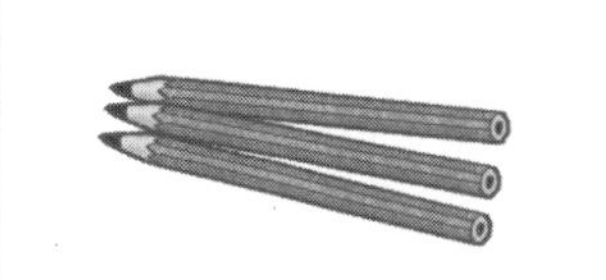

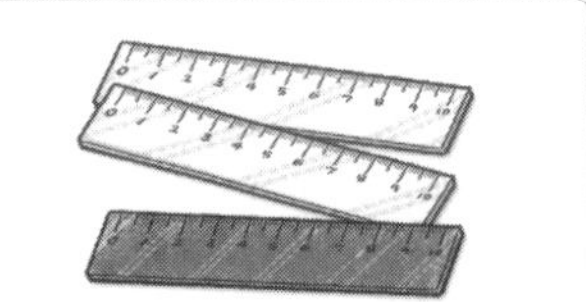

(2)

How many dice?

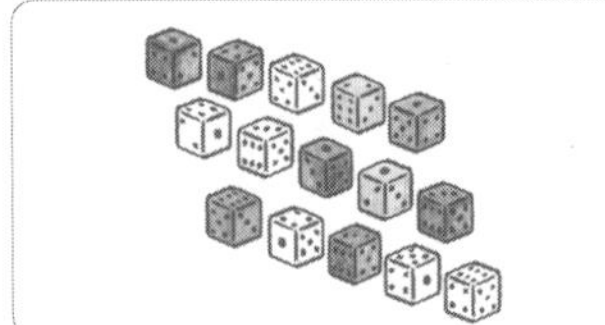

(3)

How many erasers?

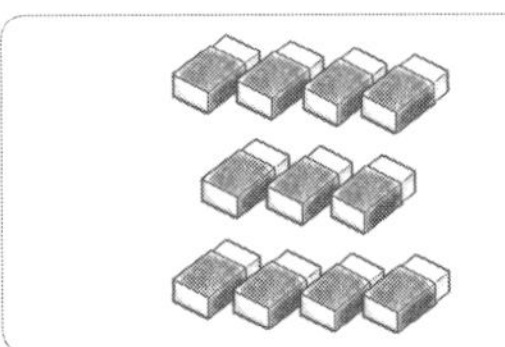

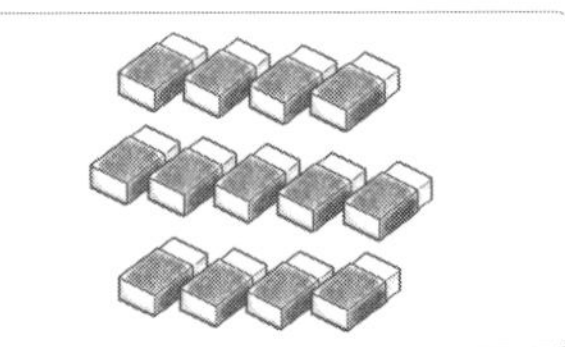

(4)

How many marbles?

2 対話を聞いて，読まれた数を□に数字で書き，あっているイラストと線でむすびましょう。

(1) □ ・ 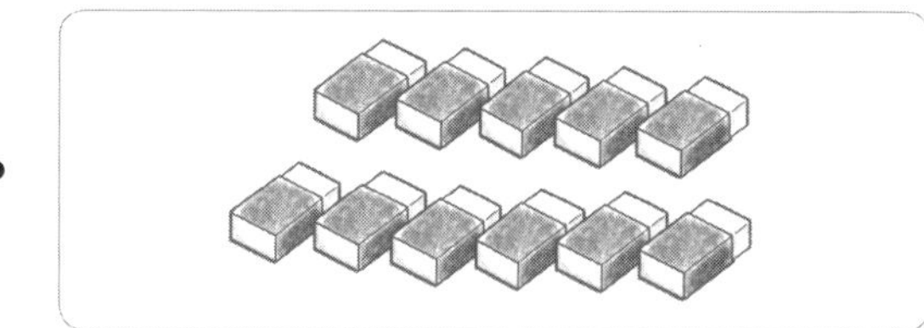

(2)  ・ 

(3)  ・ 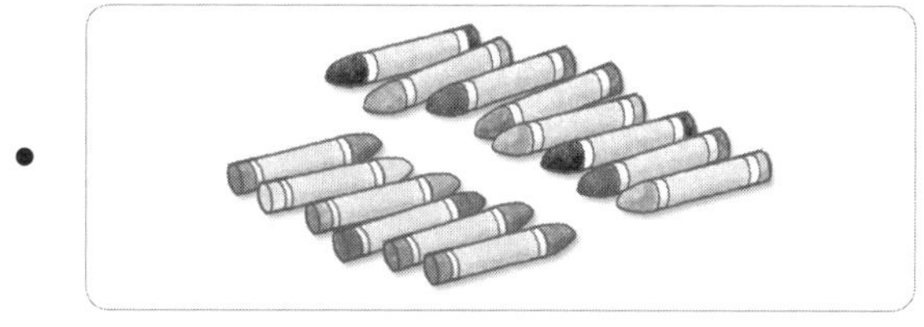

(4)  ・ 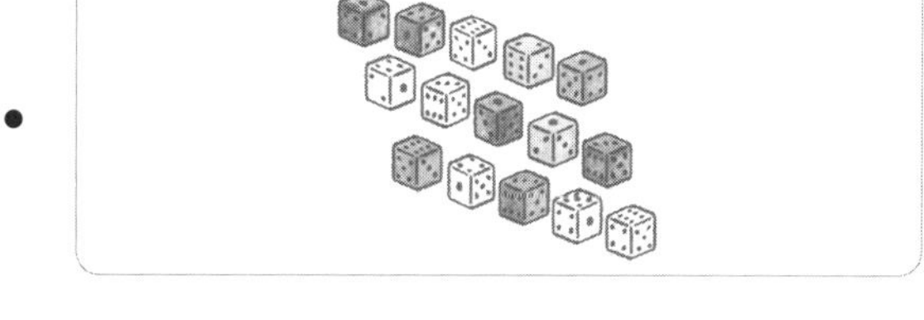

(5)  ・ 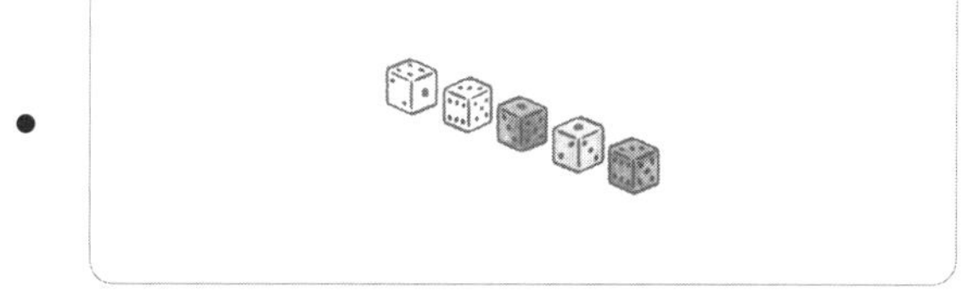

(6)  ・ 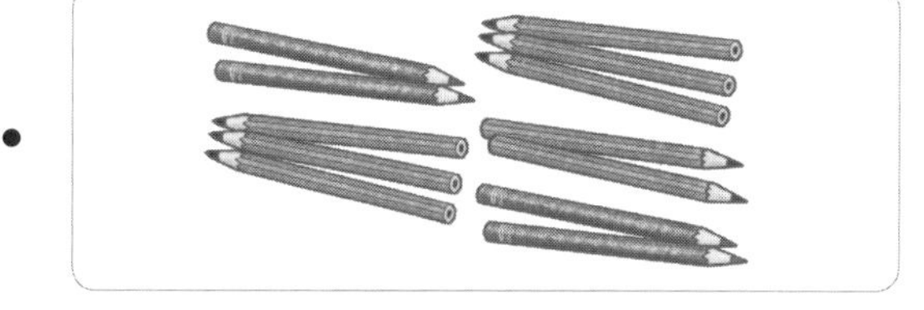

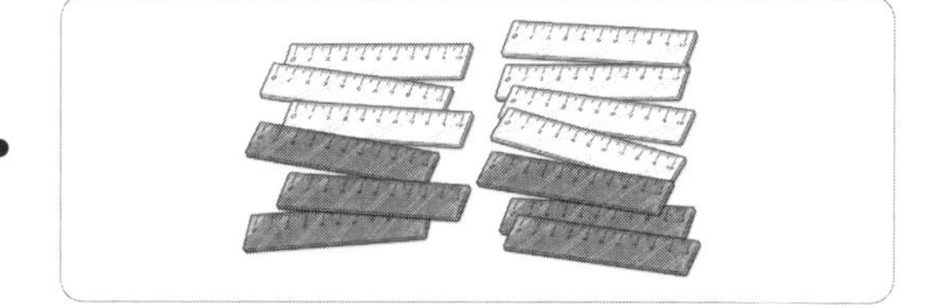

① 英語を聞いて，読まれた順番を□に数字で書きましょう。

② 英語を聞いて，読まれた順番を□に数字で書きましょう。

Open your textbook.

Put your textbook away.

Give me five!

Close your textbook.

Take out your textbook.

Give me ten!

3
英語を聞いて，アルファベットの大文字を書きましょう。
CD5 23
K
L
M
N
O
4
英語を聞いて，読まれた順にアルファベットの大文字を書きましょう。
CD5 24
1
2
3
4
5
6

Unit 4

I like blue.

対話を聞いて，たずねられた色が好きなら **Yes, I do.** きらいなら **No, I don't.** の□に✓をつけましょう。

(1)

Do you like yellow?

□  Yes, I do.
I like yellow.

□  No, I don't.
I don't like yellow.

---

(2)

Do you like orange?

□  Yes, I do.
I like orange.

□  No, I don't.
I don't like orange.

---

(3)

Do you like purple?

□  Yes, I do.
I like purple.

□  No, I don't.
I don't like purple.

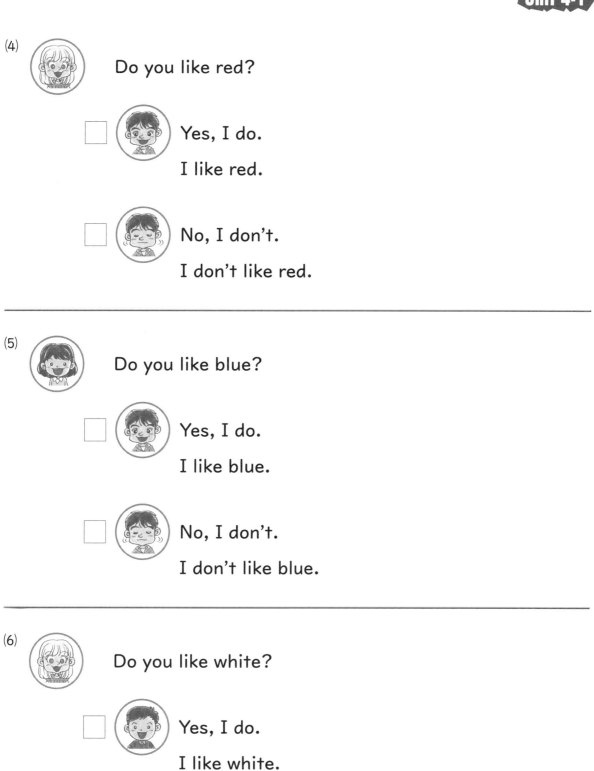

(4)  Do you like red?

☐  Yes, I do.
I like red.

☐  No, I don't.
I don't like red.

---

(5)  Do you like blue?

☐  Yes, I do.
I like blue.

☐  No, I don't.
I don't like blue.

---

(6) 
Do you like white?

☐ 
Yes, I do.
I like white.

☐ 
No, I don't.
I don't like white.

1 英語を聞いて，読まれた順番を□に数字で書きましょう。

(1)

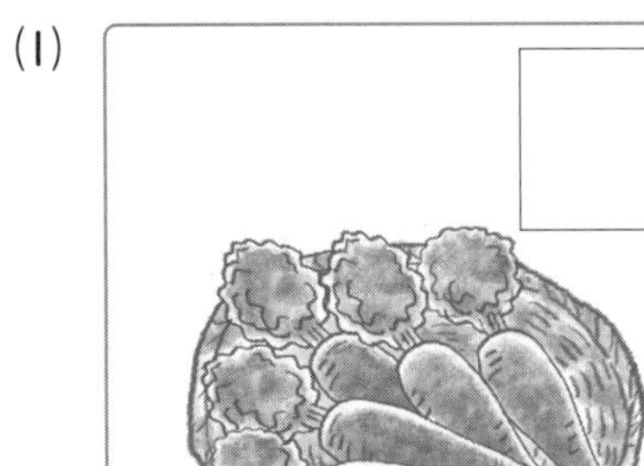

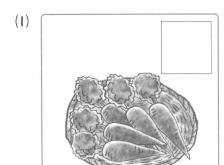

carrots

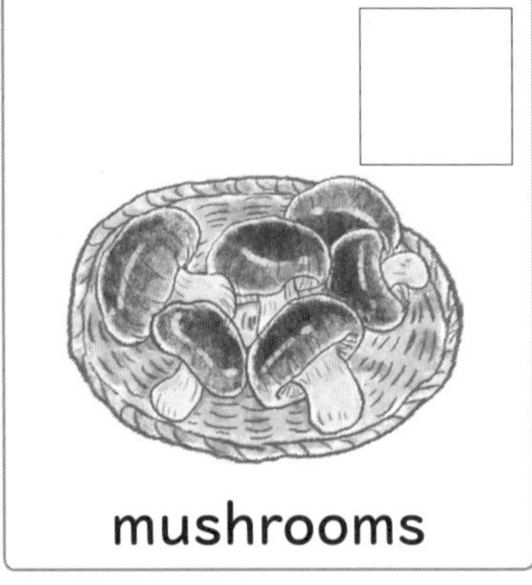

mushrooms

green peppers

(2)

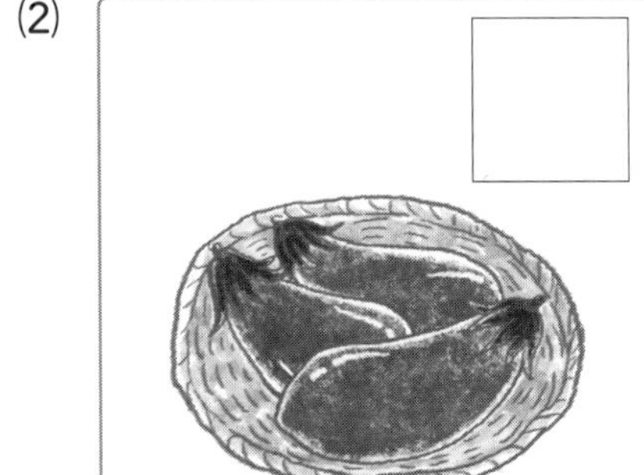

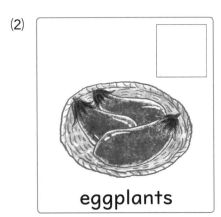

eggplants

pumpkins

tomatoes

(3)

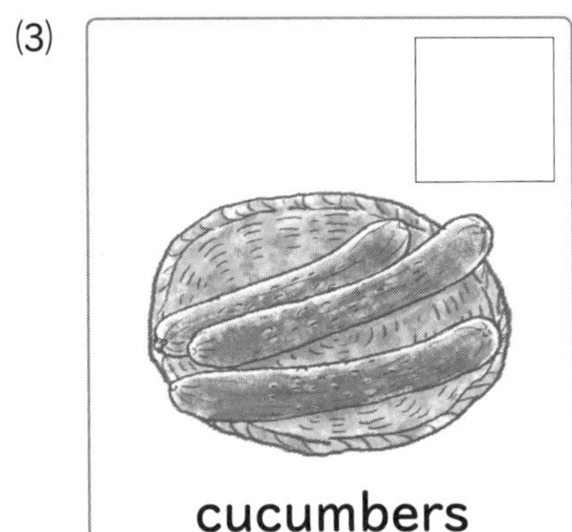

cucumbers

sweet potatoes

onions

(4)

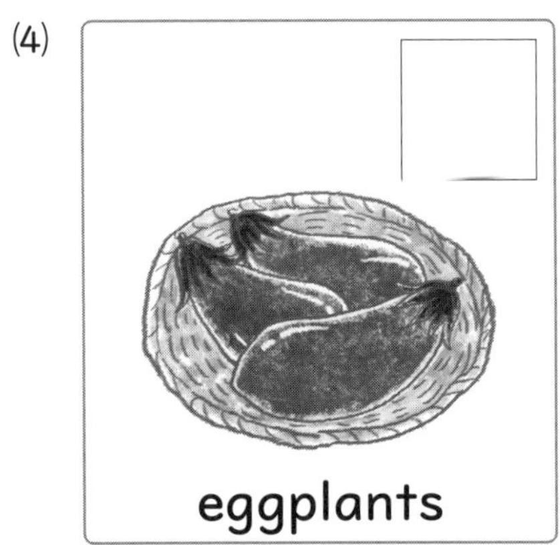

eggplants

onions

green peppers

2 対話を聞いて，それぞれが好きな野菜(やさい)には○を，苦手(にがて)な野菜には×を下の表(ひょう)に書きましょう。

	❶	❷	❸	❹

1 英語を聞いて，読まれた順番を□に数字で書きましょう。

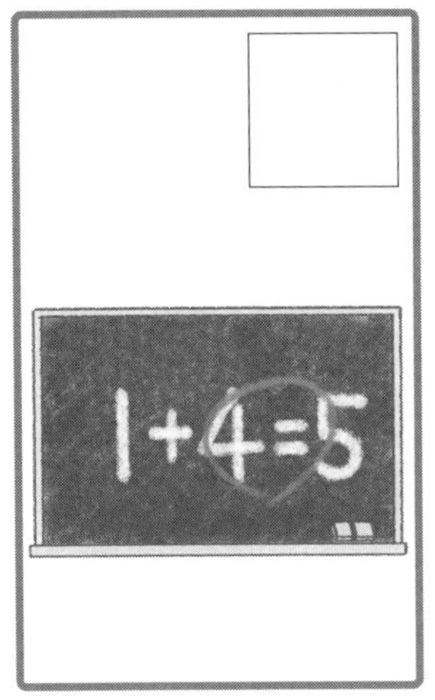

2 英語を聞いて，読まれた順番を□に数字で書きましょう。

Trace the letters.

Draw a picture.

Pick up your pencil.

Write the letters.

Put your pencil down.

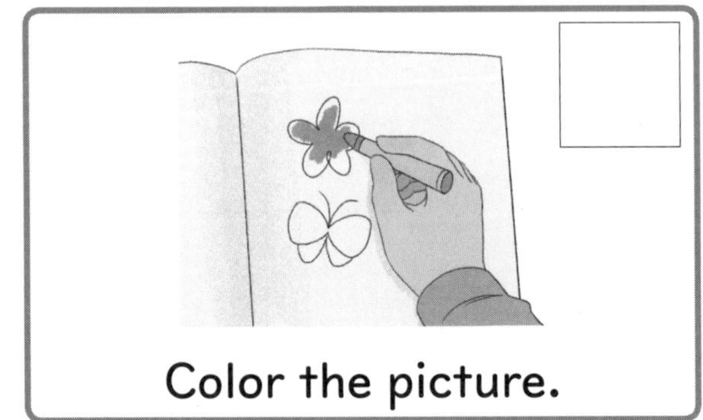
Color the picture.

3
英語を聞いて，アルファベットの大文字を書きましょう。
CD5 30
P
Q
R
S
T
4
英語を聞いて，読まれた順にアルファベットの大文字を書きましょう。
CD5 31
1
2
3
4
5
6

Unit 5

What food do you like?

英語を聞いて，読まれた順番を□に数字で書きましょう。

ice cream

bread

cheese

hamburgers

fried chicken

pizza

chocolate

rice

pudding

sandwiches

noodles

spaghetti

対話を聞いて，それぞれが好きな食べ物に○をつけましょう。

What food do you like?

I like 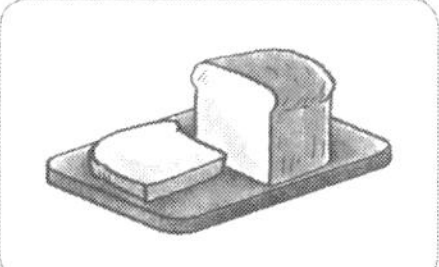   .

What food do you like?

I like  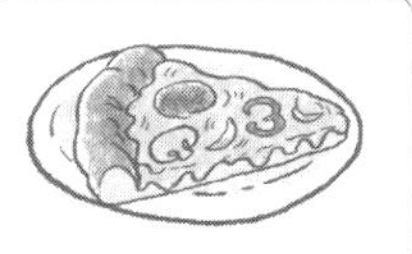 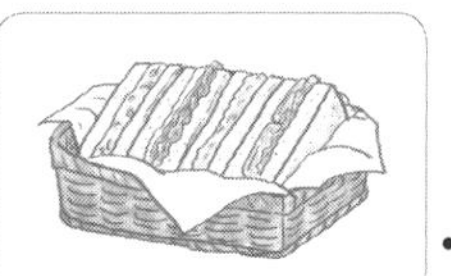 .

---

(2)

What food do you like?

I like    .

What food do you like?

I like   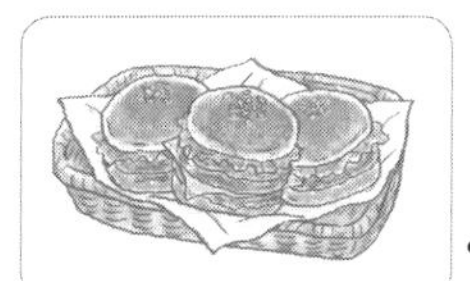 .

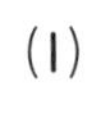

英語を聞いて，読まれた順番を□に数字で書きましょう。

(1)

apples

pears

persimmons

(2)

bananas

strawberries

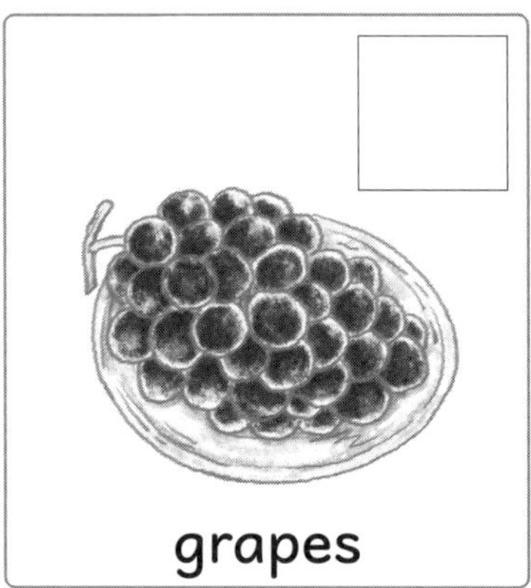

grapes

(3)

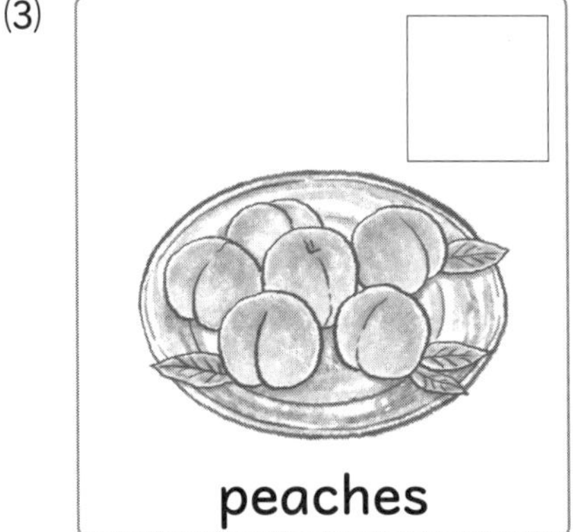

peaches

cherries

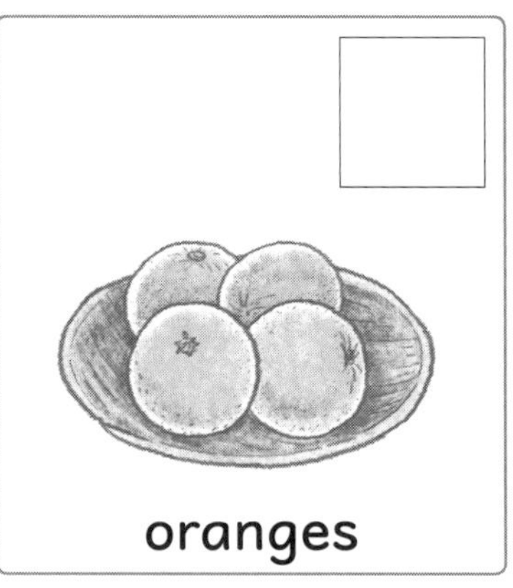

oranges

(4)

persimmons

pears

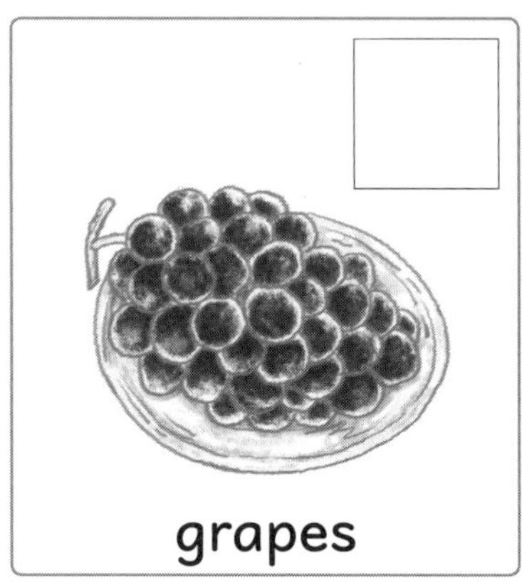

grapes

対話を聞いて，それぞれが好きな果物(くだもの)に○をつけましょう。

(1)

What fruit do you like?

I like    .

What fruit do you like?

I like    .

---

(2)

What fruit do you like?

I like    .

What fruit do you like?

I like    .

① 英語を聞いて，読まれた順番を□に数字で書きましょう。

② 英語を聞いて，読まれた順番を□に数字で書きましょう。

Look at the picture.

Open your textbook.

Show me your picture.

Draw a picture.

Point to the letter A.

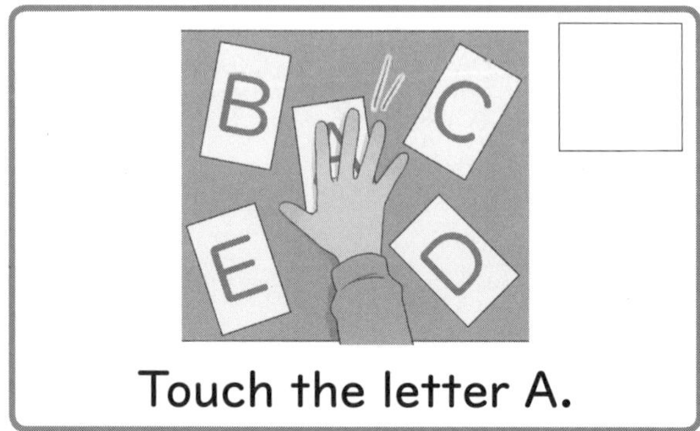

Touch the letter A.

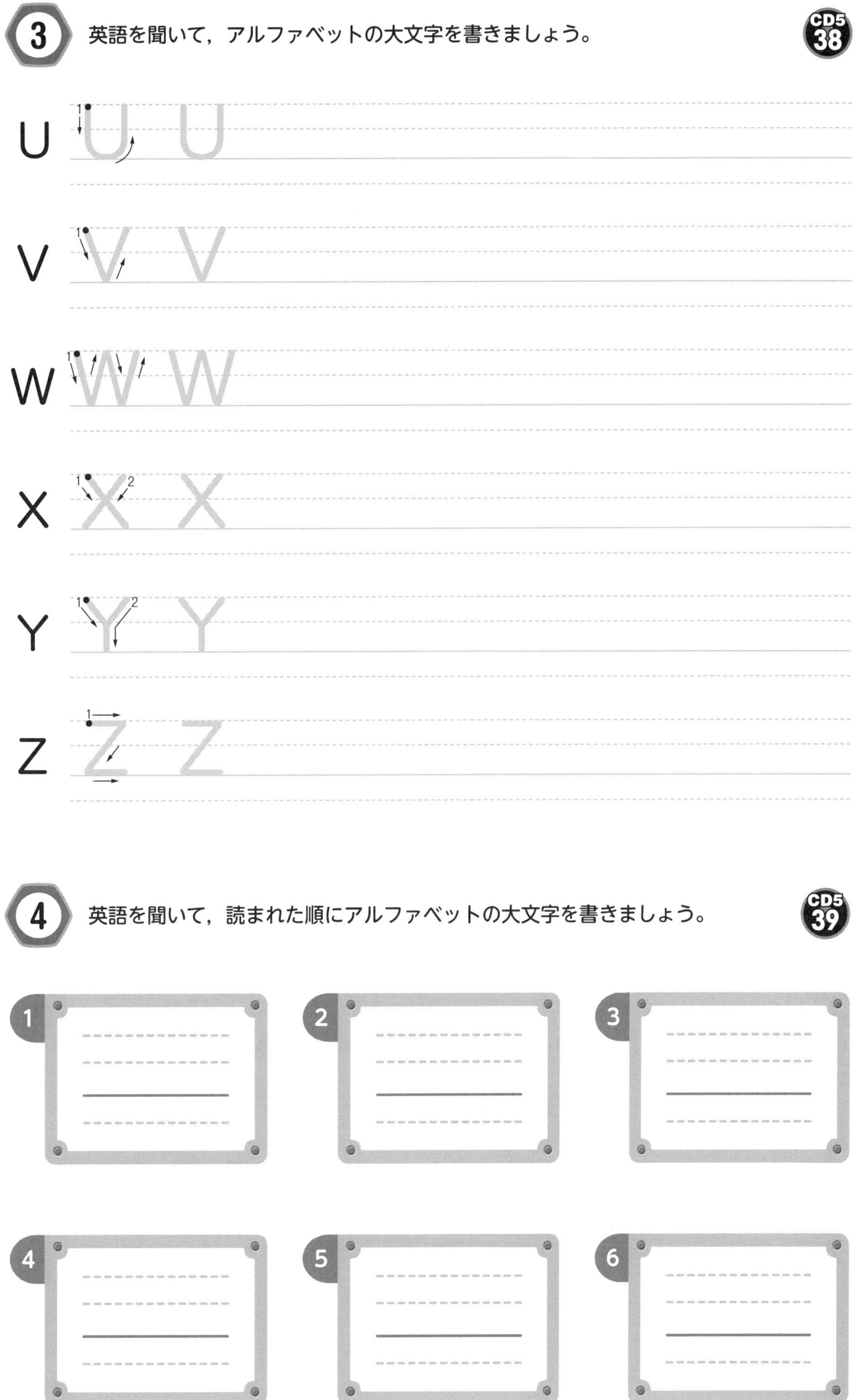

3 英語を聞いて，アルファベットの大文字を書きましょう。
CD5 38
U
V
W
X
Y
Z
4 英語を聞いて，読まれた順にアルファベットの大文字を書きましょう。
CD5 39
1
2
3
4
5
6

Unit 6

Numbers and the Alphabet

英語を聞いて，読まれた文字をなぞり，Number Chart を完成(かんせい)させましょう。

Number Chart

1 ONE	2 TWO	3 THREE
4 FOUR	5 FIVE	6 SIX
7 SEVEN	8 EIGHT	9 NINE
10 TEN	11 ELEVEN	12 TWELVE

32ページの Number Chart を見ながら対話を聞いて，答えの数字を書き，その数を表す文字を○でかこみましょう。

(1)

Look at No. 11. How many letters can you see?

 letters.

(ONE , TWO , THREE , FOUR , FIVE , SIX)

---

(2)

Look at No. 7. How many letters can you see?

 letters.

(ONE , TWO , THREE , FOUR , FIVE , SIX)

---

(3)

Look at No. 9. How many letters can you see?

 letters.

(ONE , TWO , THREE , FOUR , FIVE , SIX)

---

(4)

Look at No. 10. How many letters can you see?

 letters.

(ONE , TWO , THREE , FOUR , FIVE , SIX)

1 英語を聞いて，読まれた順番を□に数字で書きましょう。

2 対話を聞いて，読まれた時刻(じこく)をしめす時計(とけい)に○をつけましょう。

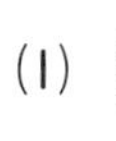

(1)  What time is it?

 It's 5:52 5:55 .

---

(2)  What time is it?

 It's 7:12 7:26 .

---

(3)  What time is it?

 It's 8:23 8:37 .

---

(4)  What time is it?

 It's 6:07 6:57 .

---

(5)  What time is it?

 It's 

11:50 .

---

(6)  What time is it?

 It's 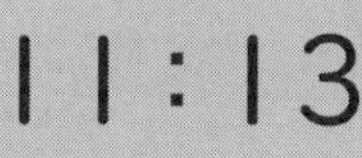

11:30 .

英語を聞いて，読まれた順番を□に数字で書きましょう。

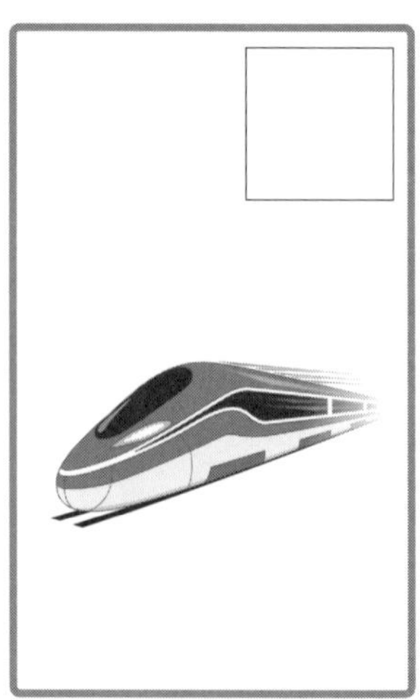

2 英語を聞いて，読まれた順番を□に数字で書きましょう。

Speak up, please.

Stand up, please.

Sit down, please.

Listen up.

Listen carefully.

Please be quiet.

英語を聞いて，A から Z まで線でむすびましょう。

Unit 7

This is for you.

1 英語を聞いて，グリーティングカードの文字をなぞりましょう。
⑷と⑸は読まれた文字を＿＿に書いて，カードを完成させましょう。

(1)

(2)

(3)

(4)

(5)

(6)

(7)

① 英語を聞いて，読まれた順番を□に数字で書きましょう。

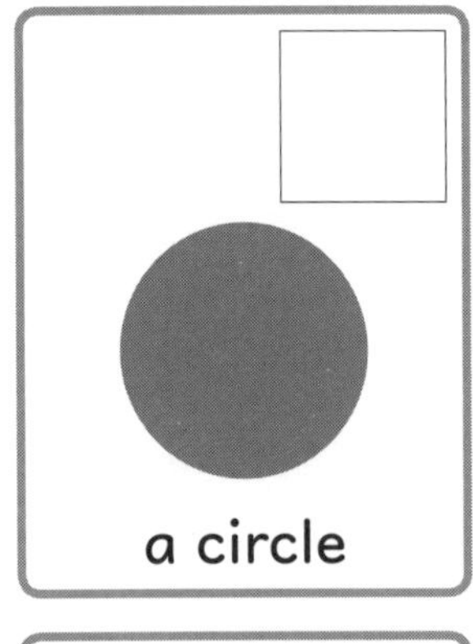

a circle

a triangle

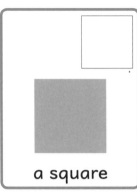

a square

a rectangle

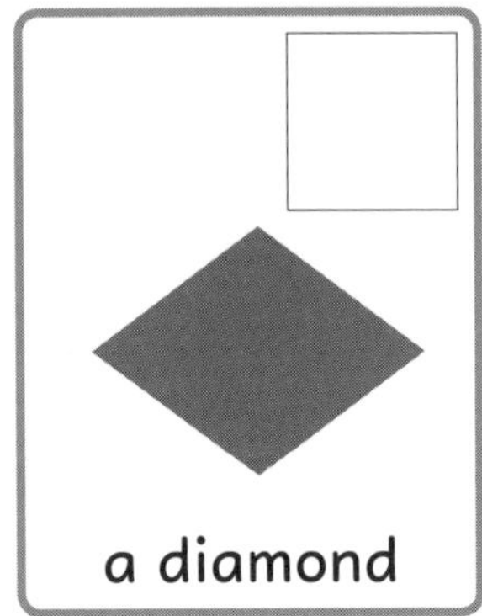

a diamond

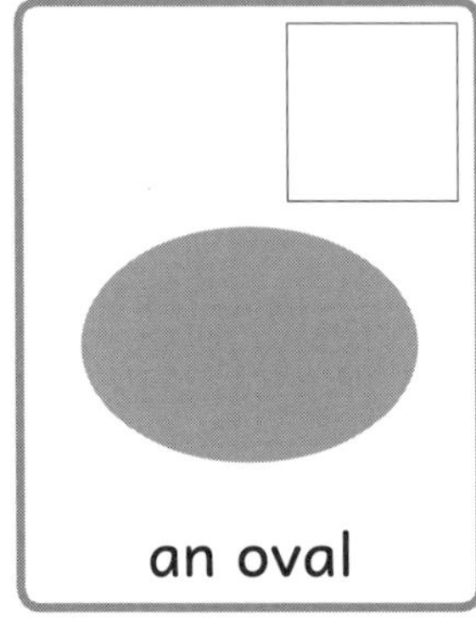

an oval

a star

a heart

② 英語を聞いて，読まれた数の図形を書きましょう。

(1)	(2)	(3)	(4)
(5)	(6)	(7)	(8)

対話を聞いて，それぞれの人物と作った作品（さくひん）を線でむすびましょう。

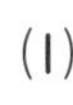
(1)

(2)

(3)

(4)

英語を聞いて，読まれた順番を□に数字で書きましょう。

2 英語を聞いて，読まれた順番を□に数字で書きましょう。

Sit down, please.

Let go of your hands.

Stand up, please.

Make pairs.

Hold hands.

Make a circle.

英語を聞いて，A から Z までの大文字を に書きましょう。

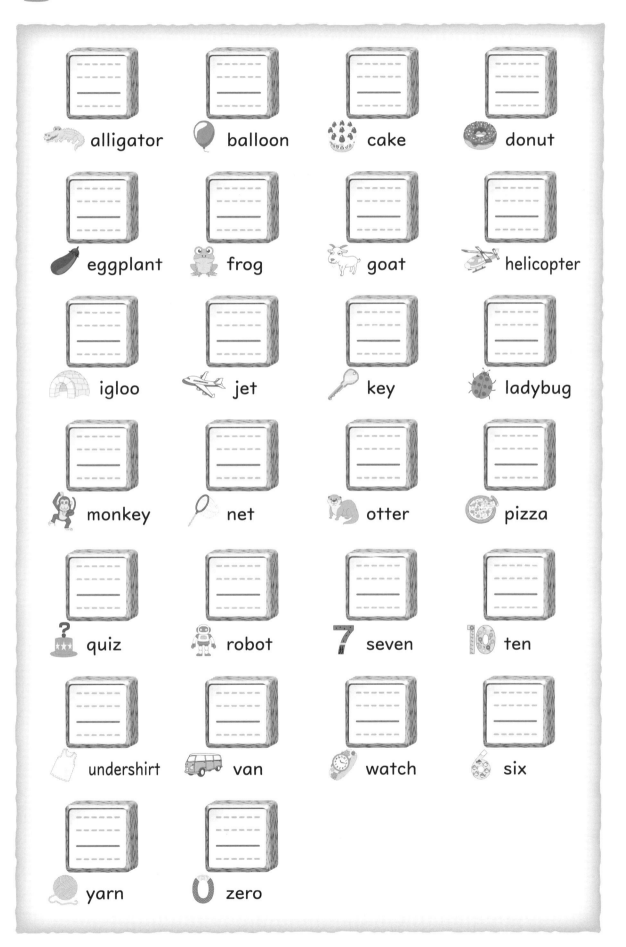

alligator	balloon	cake	donut
eggplant	frog	goat	helicopter
igloo	jet	key	ladybug
monkey	net	otter	pizza
quiz	robot	seven	ten
undershirt	van	watch	six
yarn	zero		

Unit 8

What's this?

英語を聞いて，読まれた順番を□に数字で書きましょう。

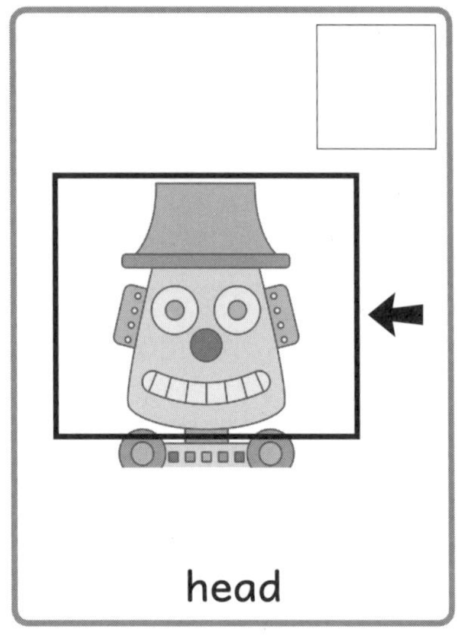

head

face

neck

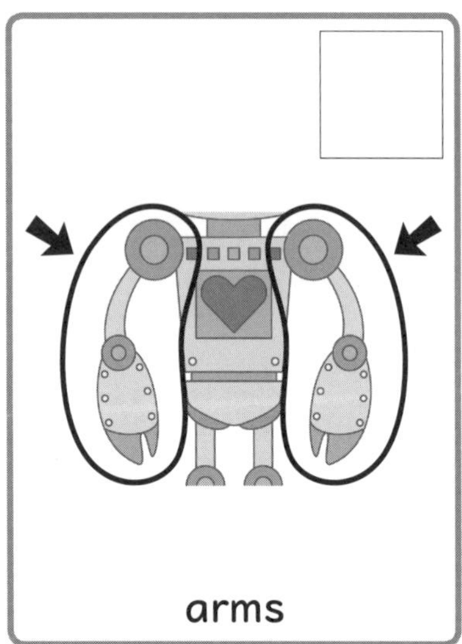

arms

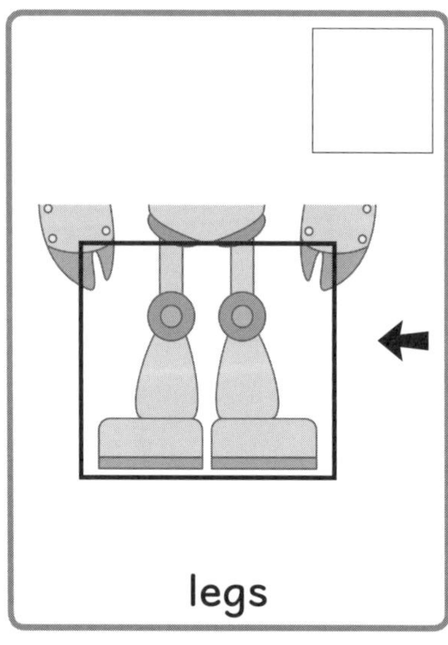

legs

eyes

ears

nose

mouth

対話を聞いて，読まれた体の部分(ぶぶん)に○をつけましょう。

(1)

What's this?

It's a   .

(2)

What's this?

It's a   .

(3)

What's this?

It's a   .

(4)

What are these?

They're 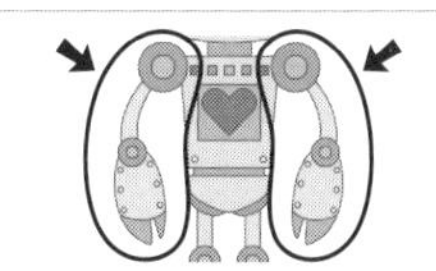 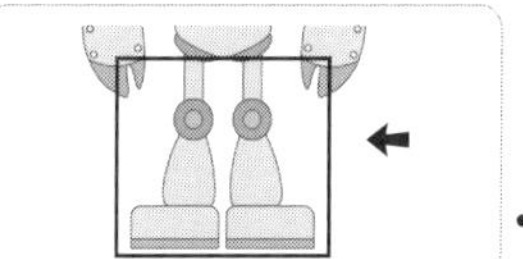 .

(5)

What are these?

They're   .

1 英語を聞いて，読まれた順番を□に数字で書きましょう。

the sheep

the tiger

the dog

the dragon

the monkey

the ox

the horse

the wild boar

the mouse

the snake

the rooster

the rabbit

対話を聞いて，読まれた干支（えと）に○をつけましょう。

 What's this? 

 It's    .

---

(2)

 What's this? 

 It's    .

---

(3)

 What's this? 

 It's    .

---

(4)

 What's this? 

 It's    .

1 英語を聞いて，読まれた順番を□に数字で書きましょう。

2 英語を聞いて，読まれた順番を□に数字で書きましょう。

Make pairs.

Make a circle.

Make a line.

Face each other.

Ask each other.

Make two lines.

英語を聞いて，干支の動物を表す英語をさがして，（　　）で囲みましょう。

U	W	N	G	Y	B	F	L	W	N	O	B
A	J	I	K	J	V	I	W	Q	J	G	S
E	H	V	I	B	D	P	I	V	F	H	N
C	O	H	G	Y	S	F	L	M	U	C	A
D	R	E	A	U	O	U	D	R	M	U	K
S	S	P	D	V	Q	F	B	A	O	O	E
R	E	R	X	W	W	P	O	P	N	Q	G
L	R	A	B	B	I	T	A	T	K	T	J
O	D	O	G	E	V	B	R	F	E	M	F
R	O	O	S	T	E	R	Q	J	Y	H	M
J	I	W	G	T	I	G	E	R	B	K	L
B	F	K	B	N	P	W	S	H	E	E	P
F	N	O	W	D	R	A	G	O	N	N	O
C	B	W	K	D	M	O	U	S	E	K	X

1 

MOUSE

2 

OX

3 

TIGER

4 

RABBIT

5 

DRAGON

6 

SNAKE

7 HORSE

8 

SHEEP

9 

MONKEY

10 

ROOSTER

11 

DOG

12 

WILD BOAR

Unit 9

Who are you?

1 英語を聞いて，あっているイラストと線でむすびましょう。 CD5 61

(1) I see something white and furry. •

• 

(2) I see something long and white. •

• 

(3) I see something long and shiny. •

• 

(4) I see something little and gray. •

• 

(5) I see something tall and red. •

• 

 対話を聞いて，あっているイラストに○をつけましょう。 

CD5 62

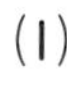

(1)  Who are you? Are you a rabbit?

 Yes, I am. I'm a   .

(2)  Who are you? Are you a snake?

 Yes, I am. I'm a   .

---

(3)  Who are you? Are you a sheep?

 Yes, I am. I'm a   .

---

(4)  Who are you? Are you a mouse?

 Yes, I am. I'm a   .

---

(5)  Who are you? Are you a rooster?

 Yes, I am. I'm a   .

1 英語を聞いて，読まれた順番を□に数字で書きましょう。

(1)

a whale

a lizard

a turtle

(2)

a squirrel

a monkey

a wild boar

(3)

a dog

a pig

a cat

(4)

a horse

an ox

a tiger

対話を聞いて，**Yes** または **No** のルートをえらび，ゴールまで進みましょう。

START

Yes Yes

No No No

Yes Yes

No No No

Yes Yes

No No

Yes Yes

GOAL

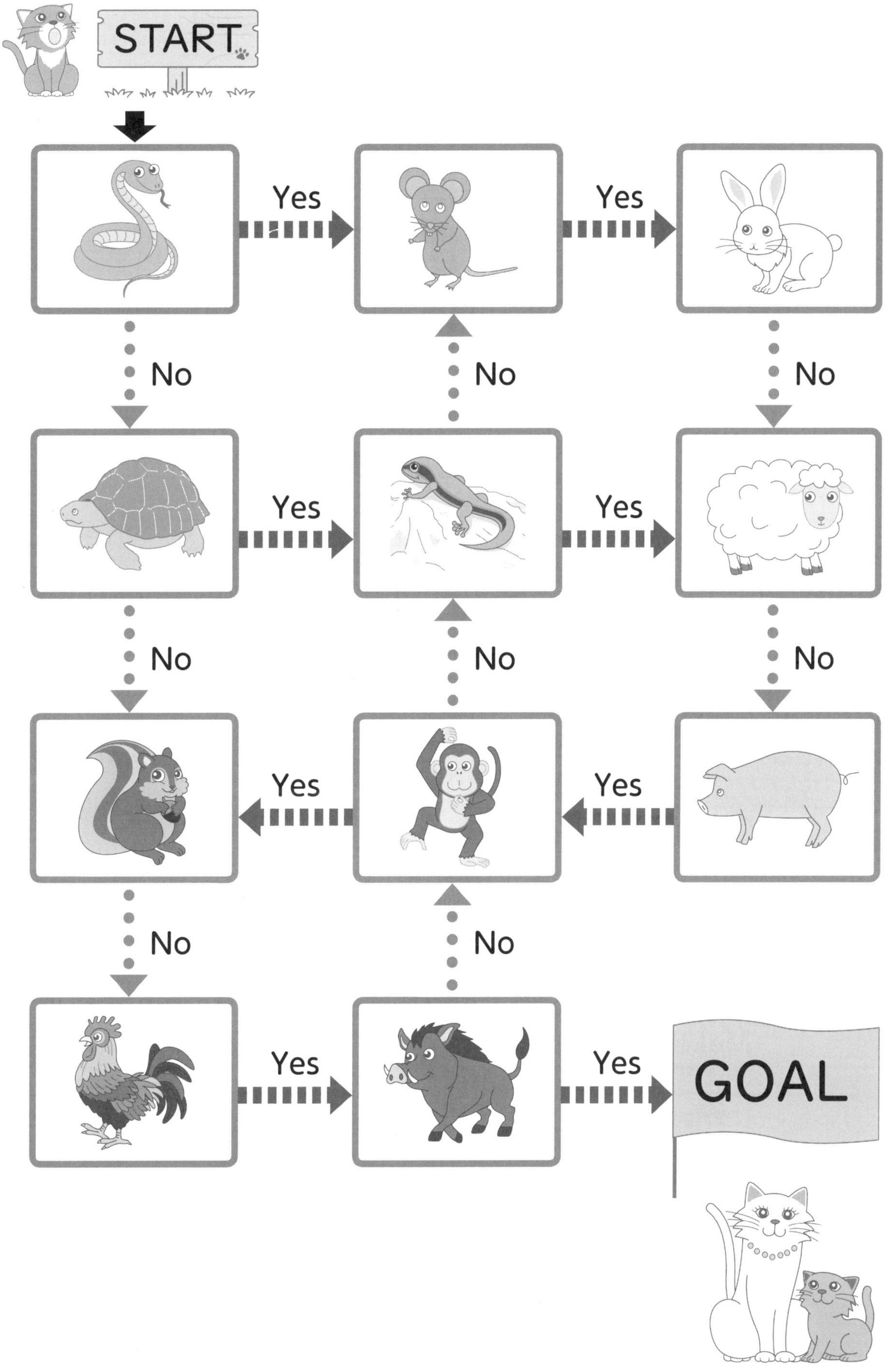

英語を聞いて，読まれた順番を□に数字で書きましょう。

2 英語を聞いて，読まれた順番を□に数字で書きましょう。

Take a step to the left.

Take a step forward.

Make a line.

Take a step back.

Make two lines.

Take a step to the right.

3 大文字で自分の名前を書いて，A から Z まで大文字を書きましょう。

Name:

1

2

3

4

5

6

7

8

9

10

11

12

13

14

15

16

17

18

19

20

21

22

23

24

25

26

Score

/26

英語でできるようになったことに✓を入れよう！

- □ 自己紹介のあいさつのしかたがわかる
- □ スポーツの言い方がわかる

- □ 気持ちや状態について会話できる
- □ 食べ物や飲み物の言い方がわかる

- □ 1～20までの言い方がわかり、足し算・引き算の問題を出しあうことができる
- □ 文房具の言い方がわかる

- □ 好きな色について会話できる
- □ 野菜の言い方がわかる

- □ 好きな食べ物について会話できる
- □ 果物の言い方がわかる

- □ アルファベットの大文字が読める
- □ 時刻の言い方がわかる

- □ グリーティングカードをわたすときのやりとりができる
- □ 図形の言い方がわかる

- □ 体の部分について会話できる
- □ 十二支の動物の言い方がわかる

- □ 短い話を聞いて、おおよその内容がわかる
- □ 動物当てクイズができる

小学 3 年

Workbook

クラス	名前

WB・A